Memoirs Of a Real life P.I.

By
H. Walter Flindt

Copyright 2008 H. Walter Flindt
978-1-4357-4387-8

Forward:

This is a book of stories, true stories of my twenty five plus years as a practicing professional private detective. Some of these stories are funny, some are scary and others are hopefully entertaining. Only the names have been changed to protect the guilty. Sit back and enjoy this inside look at my chosen profession.

About the author:

H. Walter Flindt is president of H.W.F. Services, Inc., and is a veteran Investigator with over twenty five years of experience in all types of civil and criminal cases. He has been featured on several Atlanta television news programs, the Atlanta Journal /Constitution and several magazine articles. Mr. Flindt is a recognized expert in his field and has served the Georgia Board of Private Detectives and Security Agencies as a subject matter expert.

Copyright 2008 H. Walter Flindt
All rights reserved
978-1-4357-4387-8

Dedication

This book is dedicated to the two people whom I love and adore with all my heart. First to my wife Casey who has stood by me and supported me in all the crazy things I've done. Her love, kindness, understanding, tenderness and support has helped me immensely thru the last twenty years and she has truly made me a better person. I cherish her and am so proud of the person she has become.

To my daughter Candice who has brought me joy and hope since the first second I laid eyes on her. Her trust and belief in me is worth more to me than all the riches in the world. I am truly blessed to have her love and adoration.

Contents

My very first case	7
The joy's of South Georgia	9
The friendly guy in Columbus	11
Taking a dip in the pool	12
Hiding in plain sight	13
Don't do stupid stuff	14
The eve of Christmas Eve	15
Where the deer and the antelope play	16
Sometimes aerial reconnaissance isn't enough	17
Gotta love the security guards bosses	18
Bad cop and his stupid neighbor	19
There's no place quite like Tunnel Hill	20
Don't feed the horses	21
How much stolen stuff can you get in your attic	22
Attack of the killer turtle	23
How long can you live in the back of a truck	24
Who needs a car alarm	25
Who should I shoot first	26
The not so covert camera installation	27
Sorry, I didn't know it was you	28
Babysitting 4.5 million back to Atlanta	29
Surviving South Georgia	30

Damn, that's got to suck	31
The crazy client	32
You're not my uncle	33
It's a miracle!	34
I should have brought a bigger gun	35
Bulldog has a strange sense of humor	36
I really hated having to do it	37
At least they'll know what happened	38
Air America's final revenge	39
Splat, there goes that case	40
There's always one asshole sheriff	41
I wish I hadn't done that	42
The crate	43
The package and the crazy guy	44
Oh crap, can you give me a hand	45
Home sweet ditch	46
Greed will do you in	47
Crazy drunk lady at the VFW	48
Hunting for the hunter's	49
Gee, no wonder he didn't go back to work	50
The computer take down	51
How to get a confession	52
Intercept in Tampa	53

You're going to pay for that	54
Be careful when you bend over in Dalton	55
Take your gun when you go pee	56
I wouldn't have done that if I were you	57
Be prepared	58
Hanging by a thread	59
Nothing you can do, but hide	60
Open the window first	62
The really helpful realtor	63
That will make you keep your head down	64
His wife didn't have a clue	65
Psycho lady	66
The aerial recon that almost ended badly	67

My very first case

After leaving the employment of Uncle Sam, I secured employment with a prominent Orthopedic Surgeon as a Physicians Assistant in 1979. One of my long term patients whom became a friend was going thru a nasty divorce. Thru conversations over the months of his treatment he learned of my background and asked me for help. I'll call him Bob. Bob was a sixties sort of guy and a college professor. He was a real laid back, liberal sort of fellow, except when it comes to affairs of the heart. It changed him for the worst.

Bob had married his wife, we'll call her Betty, just a year before and she was about half his age. Everything started out wonderfully, but in a matter of months Bob started to notice a strange sense of distance. She insisted that it was just that she was feeling overburdened with her work and school. To Bob this seemed plausible because she was always at work or school, so he didn't worry about it. However, as time went by he started catching her in little lies that she would always try to laugh off or change the subject. The final straw came when she just disappeared for two days without a trace, only to come home like nothing was wrong and claim to have been at a "friends" house and had simply needed some down time.

Bob called me the next morning and I agreed to meet him later that day at a restaurant in downtown Atlanta. As I entered the establishment I saw Bob at the bar and had a seat. He proceeded to describe to me in great detail what had been going on with Betty and his suspicions as to what he thinks she's really up to. After several hours, I managed to get all the pertinent information regarding Betty's work and school schedules and all of her known family and friends and assured Bob I would look into it the following week.

Bright and early the following Monday morning I did my first ride by of their residence and realized that due to the layout of the area, I would have to assume a surveillance position at the entrance to the subdivision and wait for her to depart in her vehicle. After a while Bob departed the area on his way to work, so I knew she would be leaving soon or so I thought. Bob told me that she always leaves for work twenty to thirty minutes after he leaves, so after an hour I decided to make a ride by of their house and sure enough her car is still there. I returned to my position and proceeded to patiently wait. At about 10 AM I did another ride by and saw no changes, so I called it a day and headed home.

Next morning everything went as planned. Bob leaves, then Betty Leaves and goes on about her day, just as she is supposed to. Wednesday and Thursday are a carbon copy. I conferred with Bob by phone and he told me that she led him to believe that she went to work on Monday as usual, but nothing else unusual.

There is something about Fridays I always love and it is often my lucky day. Bob leaves on schedule, but Betty is still there at 10:30 AM, so I decide to just wait patiently. I ride by the house again about noon and to my surprise there's another vehicle parked in the driveway. I quickly pull into a neighbor's driveway and try to be inconspicuous as possible. After about an hour the front door opens and out walks Betty, clad in a lace robe and her apparent friend who is the biggest African American male I had ever seen. I immediately started snapping stills as they kissed and he then entered his vehicle. I had seen enough, so I departed the area after retrieving his tag number.

The following week proved to be very enlightening. It turned out that Betty's friend was also her boss and that apparently she had been "working from home" for him on a regular basis. Must have been some special "dictation" that needed to be done. It was further revealed that he was also married and had two kids at of his own. Bob was enraged at this news. I don't know if it was because she was betraying him or the fact that her lover was African American, but he became another person. He was totally consumed with this affair and drank and drugged himself into a very dark place. He even got to the point that he asked me to kill her. I of course told him not no, but Hell No and that I was officially Betty's new guardian angel. Yes she betrayed him, but no one deserves that.

During the divorce proceedings Betty's boss was subpoenaed to court and his wife found out about his affair. Three day's later his wife shot him twice, however he survived. Bob and Betty went their separate ways, but Bob never got over it. It turned him into a vindictive, hateful old man who finally shut everyone out of his life and died alone. He never realized that you must always continue on to bigger and better things.

The joy's of South Georgia

Back in the early eighties the agency I was working for was involved in a huge fraud investigation centering on a prominent South Georgia family. They pretty much ran the town where they lived and owned most of the businesses in and around town and one of them was the mayor and yet another was the chief of police. The family also had a commercial Shrimping business just outside of Brunswick, Georgia. We'll just call them the Bubbas.

Apparently, even though they were raking in a healthy living for years and they had enjoyed a lavish life style, things were starting to close in on them. Two bad Shrimping seasons back to back and a general down turn in the local economy over the past few years had turned them into desperate people. Buildings started to mysteriously burn to the ground allegedly full of expensive inventory and heavy equipment, motor homes, even two shrimp boats vanished into thin air over a two and a half year period. Oh, don't worry, everything was well insured. As a matter of fact the cumulative losses were in the millions and these people were in need of the cash. I guess when you're desperate enough your willing to do anything, including arson and insurance fraud. Now all I had to do was prove it.

The first step in this type of investigation is to identify all potential players and then start following their individual paper trails. This was, at the time very time consuming because this was pre computer and you had to physically go to each county courthouse and hand search for information on each individual. After a couple of weeks of research, tracking down leads and putting some of the pieces of the puzzle together it became quite apparent that we needed an insider who could help fill in the blanks. However, there in lies the problem, no one would talk to us, it seemed that every one who knew of the family also feared them. We kept working on the case a few weeks and I finally made contact with a feisty senior lady who was very informative. Turns out she and her family were born and raised in the Bubbas town and she didn't care for them much. She said that the merchandise allegedly lost in the fires was in a leased building and that larger items were buried with a bulldozer on a large tract of land the Bubba's leased for years from her late son. She also informed me that she actually held these leases. I of course immediately made arrangement's with her to come pick up a copy of the leases the following Thursday. This is what we needed to put together the final pieces of what really happen to all of that stuff. Little did I know what I was walking into.

I met my number two man at the office crazy early that Thursday morning because we had a five hour drive ahead of us. It was a great trip down even though it was in the heat of a South Georgia summer and the old Chevy van had no air. We talked about business and things we wanted to do, but didn't speak of the case we were on because it seemed like a slam dunk. We pulled into town, we'll call it McBeth, and tried to follow the feisty senior lady's directions, unfortunately something got screwed up. We then decided to pull into the local gas station and ask for directions to her street. I got out of the vehicle and approached the middle aged attendant. I smiled and politely asked for directions to the street. The guy just stands there and stares at me for what seems like five minutes and then asks me who I am and what am I doing in this town. I stared back at him and gruffly asked him what the fuck is it to you and walked out. I got back in the van and started it up and then told my number two that we were on our own, because the people here are assholes.

We reevaluated our directions and followed them backwards and eventually found our lady's house. Leaving my partner and my weapon in the van, I got out and went to the front door. She opened the door and let me in and we headed for the sitting room. We sat and talked a while as she explained each document to me and discussed other pieces of information she had regarding the Bubba family. I thanked her and headed to the door. As I reached for the door knob I could see thru the glass pane that there was a police car parked next to my van and the cop was talking to my partner. There were two pick-up trucks behind the patrol car loaded down with good Ol' boys with rifles and shotguns and it didn't look good to me at all. As I'm about to crap all over myself, I stuffed the documents down the back of my pants and walked directly to the van and enter the passengers door. I quickly picked up that my partner was trying to convince the cop that we were vending machine mechanics trying to get permission to place vending machines at several locations within the city. I just sat there quietly as I inched my hand towards my Smith &Wesson model 13, 357 magnum lying in the floor board. These bastards weren't kidding around and if he ordered us out of the vehicle I felt I would have no choice but to shoot the cop first and then any one who pointed a weapon our way. then try to get the hell out of there and contact The Georgia Bureau of Investigation for help. Fortunately for us the cop bought the story and escorted us not only out of town, but to the county line, good Ol' boys in tow. God I hate that place.

A week after that fun filled trip we found out that prior to our involvement in the case the G.B.I. had dispatched two agents to McBeth to investigate the same family however they disappeared without a trace until the following summer. One was stood in a wash tub and the other was placed in a fifty five gallon drum cut off at the first ring and both were filled with cement. They were then dropped in the nearby river where the bodies remained until uncovered by the severe summer drought.

Me thinks I'll just stay away from that place from now on.

The friendly guy in Columbus

Sometimes you can try everything on a case and still not get any where. Then sometimes your subject goes out of their way to bust themselves.

I received a routine assignment on a workers compensation case in Columbus, Georgia. We are often times asked to verify if a claimant is injured as badly as they say they are so I and my new guy loaded up the van and headed for Columbus.

Upon arriving on location I realized that due to the way our subject's neighborhood was laid out that we wouldn't be able to do a standard stationary surveillance because of a big risk of getting burned. We drove out of the area and retrieved my survey crew sign's and equipment from the back of the van. We then came back in and set up our operation adjacent to the subject's property.

After about an hour of trying to look busy out comes our subject. He of course is watching us work and being the friendly guy he is strolls over to chat. While we talk he takes note of the video camera on the tripod in plain view so I proceed to tell him it's the latest high tech surveyor's transit that does everything by laser and takes like ten measurements at once. I continued my tale by saying that we were trying to finish up, but we were having trouble shooting past some of the bushes in his side yard. Our subject immediately takes off to his garage, saying that he could take care of it.

Our friendly subject returns with a full size axe and proceeds hacking away at the bushes I said were in the way. As a matter of fact he chopped away at them for thirty minutes, even down on his hands and knees and we of course video taped every glorious second of it. After he finished we finished up our "measurements" and proceeded to leave. Our friendly subject invited us in for a cold beer, but we declined saying that we could get fired for drinking on the job. We laughed our asses off all the way home.

One month later our subject came to his worker's compensation hearing wearing a neck brace, back brace, a knee brace and walked with a cane. He proceeded to testify that he was in such constant pain that he could barely stand to walk or even sit. He went on and on about what terrible shape he was in after his accident and how he would never be the same. Ah, poor fella.

When I walked into the courtroom to testify, mister friendly didn't recognize me at first, but as soon as I started the video tape he gasped loudly and began to shake. After a few minutes the judge halted the hearing and began verbally blasting the subject even cursing him at times. The subject then took off all of his orthopedic appliances and walked sheepishly out of the courtroom. I just couldn't help but laugh all the way home.

Taking a dip in the pool

I had been working an insurance fraud case in the Brunswick, Georgia area for about two weeks and had discovered that my subject was quite an enterprising fellow. Not only was he defrauding an insurance company for years but he had established a pretty good drug trade in the area selling mostly pot and methamphetamines. Knowing that the local law enforcement would want proof of his activities before they would get involved, I decided to be extra cautious and do what I call "slow walking" the case. About this time his ex-wife contacted the insurance company involved and offered to provide information as she could.

I contacted her and quickly established a rapport. She agreed that she would call and pass on any useful information she came across to keep me informed. Because they had children she would have to communicate with him and he was a big talker and liked to brag. The following Friday she called me about noon and told me that she had just gotten off the phone with subject. Subject stated that he would not be able to pick up the kids this evening as planned because he had a big deal going down later that night. I headed to the house and quickly packed a few things and started the five and half hour drive to Brunswick.

When I arrived at the subject's residence, his car was still there so I found a safe place to await his departure. Shortly after 9:00 PM he left the house and headed into town stopping at the local McDonald's drive thru. After receiving his order he pulled into a parking place and parked. Thinking that he may be making his meet here I proceeded to move close to his vehicle and secured a parking space adjacent to his. Unfortunately he simply ate his big Mac and fries and then continued on his way. I kept a loose tale on him because I had to get close to him twice and was afraid he might make me. My subject finally arrived at a dance club at a popular hotel in Jekyll Island. It was the off season (November), but the locals always flocked to the place.

I noted that the club itself was all glass and it had a great view of the ocean. With it being a dark moonless night you could peer inside the club and see most everyone clearly, but they couldn't see you. I started working my way slowly around the outside of the building trying to locate my subject. As I rounded the far left corner of the club the ground just disappeared and the next thing I know is I am in a swimming pool. As I'm shaking off the effects of the freezing cold water I can hear hysterical laughter coming from a couple snuggling under a blanket at the far end of the pool. I however am furious, I'm soaking wet, freezing, drew at lot of attention upon my self and on top of that I can't go inside the club like this.

I get back to my vehicle and proceeded down the road to another hotel. As I'm walking into the lobby of the hotel I notice that I'm making a loud squishing noise with each step that I take. You should have seen the look on the desk clerks face. He never said anything about the fact that I was soaking wet, but you could sure tell he wanted to. By the time I got back to the club my subject was gone. Bummer.

Hiding in plain sight

I received an assignment on a fraud case on the outskirts of the small rural South Georgia town of Jesup. This is a sleepy quiet community with few paved roads and everyone knows each other.

As I usually do, we got into town and secured a hotel room and then proceeded to locate our subject, we'll call him Mr. Jones. After about an hour and a half search we located Mr. Jones residence way off of the main state route on a secluded single track dirt road and he was surrounded by family. We noted that he also had a large workshop and barn on the premises. I realized that we may be on a private road on private property which legally we couldn't do without permission so we left the area and proceeded to the county courthouse. Once there we proceeded to the tax assessor's office and pulled property records, plats and maps. From these we were able to determine that the road Mr. Jones lived on was indeed a county road with a public right of way on each side. Great, we could get in there legally, but how do we stay in the area long enough to run a surveillance and not get burned?

That night at dinner, my partner and I decided that the only choice we had was to try the survey crew set up under the guise of preparing to pave several roads in the area. We headed out about 9:00 AM the next morning, we usually get out a lot earlier, but we didn't know how long we would be able to stay in the area so we wanted to make sure they were up and moving before going in.

When we pulled into the area and saw the workshop doors were open and several vehicles parked in front we pulled up directly in front of the property. As my partner slowly got out and started setting up the "survey Equipment", I set up my camera and zoomed in on the workshop. It turned out that Mr. Jones was apparently a mechanic and hot rod builder. He had parts being delivered periodically and customers stopping by to pick up and drop off vehicles, but no one paid us any attention. We spent two days hovering around there videoing Mr. Jones as he worked diligently on those cool car's. He and his family would come and go and even wave to us, but apparently had no clue what was going on. Man, it's amazing how convincing a hard hat and a couple magnetic signs can be.

Don't do stupid stuff

We all do stupid things at times and sometimes they are the best life lesson's we learn. I used to love to stay out late and party with the ladies, but that and a touchy early morning surveillance don't mix.

The firm I worked for back in the eighty's had basically came to an impasse on a challenging worker's compensation case. It was believed that our subject was selling antiques out of her home which was located in a curve of a state highway in the North Georgia Mountains and was surrounded by trees. The layout was really horrible for surveillance and back in those days the tiny pinhole cameras did not exist. I noted that there was a very steep and narrow hill directly across the highway which could be accessed from the rear by a small dirt road. This would be an excellent place to set up a covert surveillance position while my partners went in and bought something. We planned it out for bright and early the following Saturday morning.

The Friday afternoon before, I was at my office working on payroll and catching up paperwork. A very hot brunette friend of mine called out of the blue and wanted to hang out so we made plans for dinner that night. After dinner we decided to go to a club and have a few drinks and dance. Somewhere between then and 6:00AM the next morning we wound up buck necked on the couch in the waiting room of my office. I'm supposed to meet my partner's there at 6:30 AM and I was still totally fried. I wake my friend up and helped her to her car and then came back in and started a pot of coffee. By the time I got my camouflage gear out of the van my partners were there. OH shit.

On the way up to the mountains, I slept the best I could in the back of my partners Blazer. When we got there we drove down the dirt road behind the hill and I got out and donned my back pack loaded down with surveillance gear. I could barely stand up on level ground, but knew I had to get up that hill. My partners proceeded to the subject's house as I scrambled and scraped my way up the hill through the thick underbrush.

As I crested the hill I was still too drunk to realize that the underbrush was much thinner on the side of the hill facing the subject's house. I saw my partners pull into the subject's driveway and get out so I tried to hurry to get in position. As our subject and her husband were speaking to my partners I catch a boot on a limb and start tumbling down the hill with my pack. When I come to a stop I realize everyone is staring at me from across the street. Realizing how badly I screwed up I start a mad scramble back up the hill. By the time I was back up at the crest of the hill I start getting a mayday call on the radio from my partner letting me know the subject's husband was headed in my direction with his gun. I radioed my partners back and had them quickly pick me up. As we flew down the dirt road we passed the irate husband in his truck and got the hell out of there.

Note to self: Don't do covert Op's Drunk.

The eve of Christmas Eve

I had a large corporate client that was experiencing an ongoing theft problem at one of their warehouse facilities in Southwest Atlanta. We had busted up a theft ring at this facility two years prior, but things were happening again. Due to additional security measures that were implemented, we were pretty sure it had to be happening at night when the facility was closed and the guards were probably involved.

I met with their head of corporate security and we devised a plan where I and one of my guy's would secretly enter the facility at quitting time and lock ourselves in a two story office structure centrally located inside the huge warehouse. All we had to do was stay low and avoid detection by the on premises security guards.

It was the eve of Christmas Eve, we met the facility manager at a side door and he let us in and walked us to the office structure. He wished us luck and locked the door. The security guards did not have keys to his office so we felt pretty comfy. About 7:00 PM most everyone was gone and the place was quiet. The first thing we noticed was the guards were not making their hourly rounds. Matter of fact we hadn't seen the first one all night.

Finally at about 2:30 AM one of the guards came into the warehouse riding a three wheel bike with a large basket. For the next hour and a half I quietly video taped the guard going from area to area going thru boxes and placing merchandise in the basket of his trike. He would fill it up and ride out of sight to the front of the building and then return to do more shopping. After he finished his Christmas shopping we never saw another guard that night. At 7:00 AM when the facility opened to employees, we let ourselves out of the office and walked out the front door past the sleeping guards. They had absolutely no clue what was going on.

Later that same day we provided a copy of the surveillance tape to the Fulton County Police Department and the night security guards were arrested when they reported for work.

Where the deer and the antelope play

In November of 1995 I was contacted by one of our corporate security clients regarding thefts at one of their warehouses even with new guards and security cameras. After sitting down and going over the circumstances surrounding the thefts with our clients we determined that the late shift was probably involved. There were only seven employees on this shift and all supervisors and management were gone, and they had access to unmonitored rear doors to the facility for maintenance purposes.

Due to the facility being located in an isolated heavily wooded area with a railroad access track passing to the rear of the facility I decided that this would be the best way to covertly approach and surveil the building. I would have one of my guys drop me off at the rail line and hike in, while my partner found a place to wait in a chase vehicle in case we needed to tail someone out.

The following Wednesday we headed out and got there at 5:30 PM so I would have time to get into position before dark. It was a fairly long walk up the tracks before I was behind our building and climbed the steep embankment into the woods. After a sixty yard stomach crawl, I moved quietly into a camouflaged position under a pine tree and did a radio check with my number two guy. As the sun went down I assembled my night vision lense onto my camera and continued to carefully scan the rear of the warehouse just waiting for one of the rear doors to open.

After several hours of staring thru binoculars at the rear of the building it was starting to get chilly and to make matters worse a light steady rain began to come down. I snuggled back against my tree and covered my gear as best I could and continued to peer at the building as the rain dripped from my jungle hat. After another hour or so in the pitch black rainy night I decided it was time for a smoke. I slowly pulled a cigarette and my lighter from the breast pocket of my jungle shirt and then set my binoculars on the ground beside me. I place the well deserved smoke in my mouth and as always cupped my hand around it so no one could see the light and lit the lighter. Holy shit, all of a sudden from behind me came a horrendous bellowing noise like Satan would make and I began being peppered with dirt and rocks. I proceed to roll away from the noise and draw my weapon. As the muzzle of my Colt 45 came free of the holster I caught a glimpse of my attacker. It was a deer. Apparently, sometime during the night the deer had bedded down on the other side of the tree and neither of us knew the other was there until I flicked my Bic. Man we scared the hell out of each other that night.

Sometimes aerial reconnaissance isn't enough

I was contacted by one of my regular clients regarding a particularly difficult multi million dollar fraud case in Chilton County, Alabama. It involved an individual that was involved in a relatively minor automobile accident and seemed fine at first however two months later claimed he was paralyzed from the waist down.

I did an initial ride by of the area and immediately realized that a standard vehicle surveillance would not work. The subject lived on top of a heavily wooded hill off of a narrow county highway in a very rural area. The front of the residence was only partially visible from the highway directly in front of the subject's property and there was no place to sit inconspicuously in a vehicle. The only option was to conduct a covert surveillance of the subject's residence if we could get access. This means that we utilize special camouflage and techniques where you literally crawl within close range of your target and set up a surveillance position in a suitable vegetated area.

My first stop was the county courthouse to research property records and determine his exact tract of land and who owns the surrounding property. I then contacted an adjacent property owner and got clearance to use his property. My final step in my preparations was to do an aerial photo reconnaissance of the property that revealed two mobile homes on the property, numerous vehicles including dune buggies and an out building. Now that I had my homework completed it was time to schedule the op.

My number two man and I went out the evening before and checked into a hotel. I then took him out to the area and showed him around so he would be familiar with the layout of the area and my planned insertion and extraction sites. In the morning I pulled my gear together and donned my ghillie suit, which is a camouflage suit used by military and law enforcement snipers and loaded up into the truck. As my number two man drove us to the insertion point I bailed out into the ditch. When he drove out of the area and I was sure no one was looking I entered the woods and began my long arduous crawl up the hill.

I finally crawled my way into position in the woods adjacent to the two trailers and settled in for the day. It was the middle of the summer and the forecasted high for the day was 103. By noon time I was completely soaking wet in my own sweat under my heavy ghillie suit and the fleas and other crawling critters were eating away at me. As I lie there patiently boiling in my own juices, the wind starts kicking up a little bit and I was enjoying it. That is until two very large rottweilers that I didn't know about caught my scent and proceeded slowly into the woods sniffing the ground. I lie there dead still so as not to give my position away and slowly work my right hand towards my Glock 26 in a shoulder holster as they start circling in the woods with their snouts to the ground.

Then as if sent from God I hear a female voice start calling the dogs. It seemed an eternity until they heeded their owner's call and walked back to the trailer. I got the hell out of there as fast as I could and radioed my number two guy to extract me. Damn that was close.

Gotta love the security guards bosses

I got a call from one of my corporate security clients about thefts from one of their facilities. They felt it was happening at night and had previously complained to the security guard company they used with no results. There was a late shift that came in at staggered times and the only way in or out of the facility was thru the front door which was always manned by the security guards. Their company manufactured computer, telephone and fax machines so they aren't easy to hide, but they sure were disappearing left and right.

I started the surveillance the following evening and picked a parking spot with a clear view of the front door of the facility, but not to close so I wouldn't be noticed. All went as normal thru the night as employees came and went. No suspicious activity from any one including the security guards. As a matter of fact it was a little boring.

On the following three nights it was the same story, employees reporting for duty and checking out and going home. One of the security guards coming out to smoke. No suspicious activity, no suspicious vehicles, no one carrying out boxes, no nothing.

I arrive on night number five and take up my favorite parking spot. After I set up my gear I got comfy in the back of my van and proceeded with my duties. Around about eleven PM a dark colored SUV bearing the security guard company logo pulled into the parking lot and proceeded to park directly in front of me. I continued my observation of the front of the building for a few minutes waiting for some one to get out of the vehicle and go in. Finally, I slowly crawled to the front of the van and slightly opened the curtain to see what was going on.

The SUV had four occupants in it, a male and a female in the front seat and another couple in the back seat and they were having a good time. I moved my camera to the front of my van and began video taping the whole thing. They were drinking beer and smoking pot as they listened to the stereo and played grab ass and boobs. The girl in the front seat was rocking hot and had a great rack, as she whipped them out several times. This went on about thirty to forty minutes and I recorded every second of it. The driver eventually got out, straightened his company shirt and went into the facility. Five minutes later he comes out and they leave.

The following morning I informed my client of the events of the night. By noon my client had cancelled a six figure contract with the security company and hired a new one. What a bunch of dumb asses.

Bad Cop and his stupid neighbor

I received a case on a local city police officer that alleged he had been injured in an on duty traffic accident. The accident itself was a minor fender bender however the cop was claiming a back injury and had been out of work for some time.

I started the surveillance early A.M. as I usually do and upon arriving in the cop's neighborhood I realized that it would be a difficult set up. It was a small tightly populated circular subdivision on the side of a hill. To be able to surveil his residence directly for any period of time would be very difficult. I noted my targets tag number and assumed a surveillance position outside the subdivision and waited for him to leave.

After a couple of hours I did a ride by of the targets residence and observed no changes nor activity so I returned to my original position. At 11:00 A.M. I did a second drive by his house and to my delight; he was out washing his car. As I drove by him he looked at me and waved and I smiled and waved back. I pulled into an empty driveway uphill from his residence and jumped in the back of the van and started filming.

I sat there for an hour and a half as he vigorously rubbed and scrubbed and then polished his car to perfection. He was bending over and squatting as he worked away on his car, but he claimed he could not even sit upright in a chair for longer than fifteen minutes. As he was finishing up his wheels it was like the hair must have stood up on the back of his neck, he turned and looked in my direction, slowly got up and walked into his residence.

As I am waiting for my target to reappear, I hear the door open to the residence where I'm parked. A male strolls out to my van and tries to look thru the tinted windows. I quickly took out my badge and opened a side window. As the guy walks around to the side with the open window, without showing my face, I thrust my badge in his face and told him to mind his own damn business. Without a word he turned around and went back inside.

A few minutes later my target came back out and finished picking up his car wash supplies and returned inside. A couple of minutes go by and an attractive blonde woman walked up the street carrying a cake and approached my target's residence. He met her at the door and they kissed and then proceeded to get into his car. They kissed again and proceeded to depart the area. I then followed them to a birthday party at a local restaurant.

As it turns out this bad cop screwed up twice on this one day. The video I recorded of him was first used at his claim hearing where he was ruled against and then fired and then a second time at his divorce hearing; see the target was married, just not to the girl on the surveillance video. When his wife saw the tape at the claim hearing she immediately filed for divorce.

There's no place quite like Tunnel Hill

In Northwest Georgia, just off I-75 is the city of Tunnel Hill. A very small community back up in the mountains and home to some interesting individuals. I found this out early in my career when I went there on an insurance investigation.

My targets residence was located on a narrow dead end dirt road on top of a mountain along with two other trailers in the immediate area. Being such an isolated area any one that didn't live there would immediately arouse the local's suspicion. After some scouting around I located an old logging road that ran up the back side of the mountain, it wasn't drivable but it was a great avenue up to the area for a covert operation.

The next morning I put on my camo jungle fatigues, packed my ruck sack and drove out to the logging road. It was at the start of dawn when I started up the trail. It was cool and crisp and I made good time up to the area and hid in the thick brush along the side of the dirt road. Now all I needed was some action.

Just before eleven A.M. the side door of my target residence opened and out came two large German Shepard Chow mix dogs and go about their business. This was all fine and dandy for about ten minutes and then they caught my scent. They started barking constantly and smelling around for me. I stayed put in the thick brush until they came in looking for me. As I was low crawling back down the hill they came into view, so I pulled out my tear gas canister and gave them a good soaking. They took off towards home wining. Clearly this approach wasn't working out to well.

About a week later I went back out on the case and decided to just go for broke and pull up in there and see how long I could stay. As I drove up to the target residence, low and behold she was out and chopping fire wood next to the drive way. She was supposed to be wheel chair bound. I waved at her and she waved at me as I drove by and parked next to the other trailers. I immediately jumped in the back of the van and set my camera up on the tripod and began filming.

After about twenty minutes I noticed one of the trailers front door slowly opened and out peered two white males. They disappeared back inside for a moment then came back out carrying shotguns. I made sure the camera was on my target and grabbed my badge and gun. As they walked up to the side of the van I slid the side door open and stuck the badge out first, followed by me and my gun. I quickly got hold of the situation and neutralized the threat. Turn's out one of the guy's was involved in a bitter divorce and he thought I was there to kidnap the child on behalf of his soon to be ex-wife.

The camera was however recording away the whole time and I got what I needed on my target. I decided I had enough of this place and headed for home.

Don't feed the horses

I received a potential insurance fraud assignment from one of my regular client's in central Alabama. The individual was claiming extensive injuries and limitations even though it was just a minor traffic accident that he had been involved in. When I got on location I immediately realized that standard vehicle based surveillance would be almost impossible, because it was on an isolated country road and there was little or no traffic except locals coming thru. Obviously a strange vehicle parked on the side of the road would stick out like a sore thumb.

I went into town and did some courthouse research and spoke with the local Sheriff's office and found out that the man who lived across the road from my subject had a distinct dislike for him. Seems the subject's dogs had repeatedly harassed, chased and even bitten one of his horses he kept on the property. I contacted this nice fella under a pretext and he gladly agreed to me using his property to surveil from. The front of his property was literally his horse pasture and about half of it was heavily wooded. The perfect place to set up a covert surveillance position to continually watch my subject.

Early the next day I carefully moved into position in the woods and set up my blind. Even though I'm in camo I like to use a ghillie net to hide my position and give me an extra layer of concealment. As the day went by I carefully documented my subject's activities as he worked on his property cutting brush and preparing an area for a garden. A one point in time he was carrying two fifty pound bags of fertilizer on his shoulders from the barn to the garden plot.

Around mid afternoon I got this strange feeling that I was being watched and looked behind me. There were three of the nice guy's horses standing in a line about fifty yards away and they were just staring at me. A few minutes later they took a few steps towards me and then stopped and watched me again. This went on for about an hour until they were standing around me sniffing around. I first tried to shoo them away but they weren't having that, they were apparently too interested in what was in my ruck sack. I had packed granola bars and amongst other things some saltine crackers and I think they were hungry. I figured I would give them a treat and they would go on their way. That was a bad idea. Those horses stuck to me like glue the entire time I was there working and would even follow me to a nearby tree when I went to pee.

I worked this case for a total of three days. Each day the horses were waiting on me to get there and tagged along every where I went. I even went as far the third day to try and fake them out with treats at the other side of the pasture, but within ten minutes they were back hanging out demanding more granola bars. Thank God my target never caught on to the gathering in the woods.

How much stolen stuff can you get in your attic

I was contacted by one of my corporate security clients regarding an ongoing theft problem at one of their warehouse and distribution centers. There were bulky items, desk top computers, complete telephone systems and other electronics coming up missing in large quantities. We immediately suspected it was one of their delivery drivers and requested a list of drivers and their assigned trucks.

Over the course of the next few weeks we would track a driver on his assigned route and watch for any deviation from the route or any other suspicious activity. This went on for some time due to the sheer number of drivers they employed. During the fourth week of the operation we got our first break. A driver (we'll call him Albert) was followed to an unscheduled stop at a residence on a dead end street near the facility. The driver was there about ten minutes and continued on his route. All trucks are secured with a serial numbered seal and he arrived at his first stop with the correct seal intact so we didn't think much of it at the time. The trucks are all personally sealed by the loading dock manager who was a twenty five year employee of the company.

During the fifth week I tracked another driver (we'll call him Bob) to the same residence. Again the driver was there approximately ten minutes and then continued on his way. Again the truck arrived at its next stop with the proper seal intact. Even though there was no sign of tampering with the seal I immediately knew this house was a place we needed to be able to watch closely the next time a driver made a stop.

The following week we concentrated our surveillance efforts on the two drivers we identified going to the house, while I had my number two man covertly set up at the house to await any interesting activity. That Thursday Albert returned to the residence. He exited the vehicle slid the uncrimped seal off the rear doors and grabbed several boxes and took them inside the residence. Another man exited the residence with Albert retrieved several more boxes from the truck and went back inside. Albert closed the trucks rear doors placed the seal back on. He then took a crimping tool from his pocket and secured it. Then Albert was on his way.

We immediately met with our clients and contacted the Fulton County Police Department. After a second meeting we put together a sting operation for the following week. We patiently followed Albert and Bob thru the week and they didn't make any drops at the house. It was excruciatingly painful waiting for them to go back to the house, but they didn't. We even thought they might be on to us and were just going to lay low until the heat was off. You never can tell in the real world.

The following Monday Albert went straight to the house. I called Fulton County on the way and we all converged at the same time. It was cool! We wound up recovering over a quarter of a million dollars worth of merchandise from the attic of the house and busted both drivers, the occupants of the residence and the loading dock manager.

Attack of the killer turtle

While working on a fraud case in Waycross, Georgia near the Okeefanokee Swamp, I spent a few days set up on an isolated sand road bordered on both sides by swamp. This was the only location in the area to wait for my target to move.

The first day out I sat up nice and early in the morning. There was a nice cool breeze and plenty of shade. By lunch time there was no breeze, no shade and the temperature was 101 degrees. But you see, that's not the bad part. For those of you that haven't spent any time in a swamp in the summer time, let me assure you it is an etymologist's dream. You are constantly being accosted by every species of big creepy crawly flying things known. I swear I have never seen so many nosey critters in my life in one place. One after the other they would either try to fly in my window or crawl in. I literally spent the day with binoculars in one hand and a rolled up news paper in the other.

The cool part of the case was the occasional wildlife that would cross or just wander down the road. The deer down there are smaller and even cuter than the regular variety found here in Georgia. They just cruised down the road without a care in the world paying me no mind. The wild hogs were another thing however, they kinda creeped me out. They came out of the swamp and started down the road. About ten yards from where I was they came to a sudden stop when they noticed me. They stood there and just stared and snorted at me. After about thirty minutes of this they finally started rummaging around a little bit and one started to wonder off. A few minutes later I realized what was going on; piggy number two was trying to sneak up from behind me. I reached down and picked up a few rocks and got up on top of the truck and started pelting piggy number two. This however only results in pissing them both off and they started charging at my truck. I then decided enough was enough and fired off a couple Of rounds from my Glock and they took off.

The last day there was fairly uneventful through the morning, I and the bugs were in our usual battle and everything else was quiet. Right after lunch I noticed this big blob crawl up onto the road some distance away. I grab my binoculars and gazed at it but still couldn't make out what it was. So I grabbed my camera, got out of the truck and walked up the road. When I got up on it I realized it was the biggest snapping turtle I have ever seen. I wanted to get some video of it to show my wife but he kept turning his back to me. I grabbed a stick out of the brush and held it in front of him to get his attention. Apparently that was the last straw; he bit onto it and spun around, released it and lunged after me. For those of you that don't know those huge snapping turtles can move very quickly for a short period of time and can easily bite off a finger or toe. Well of course I started backing up and he kept coming, slowly but he kept right after me. That turtle followed me back to my truck and when I got in he sat outside the drivers door with his head stretched up, his mouth open hissing at me. That day I learned that you don't mess with a mad turtle.

How long can you live in the back of a truck

Back in the early eighties I received an assignment on an individual that was a construction worker who allegedly was injured on the job. This guy wasn't your average Joe; he had a history of violent behavior starting with domestic violence, making threats against several people and even shooting up a work site with an Uzi machine gun. Along with his violent temper, he was also very paranoid and was constantly checking to see if he was being watched or followed. He was recently divorced and had moved into an apartment on the north side of metro Atlanta.

Taking into account all the above factors I realized that standard surveillance techniques would not work. We would have to carefully plan a way to surveil him without raising his or any one's else's suspicion. After taking a look at the layout of the apartment complex and surrounding area I came up with a plan. We would use a Hertz moving truck parked in the parking lot across the street as a stationary surveillance position to watch his apartment and have two chase vehicles's staged in each direction on the main road.

I rented a small box truck with a sliding door between the cab and the box of the truck. It was the Middle of summer so I knew I would have to come up with a way to keep cool all day in the back of the truck, so I bought a kiddie pool and went to the local ice house and bought three huge blocks of ice and wedged them in the pool. All that was left to do then was load up my surveillance gear and go park.

I pulled into the complex at about 5:00 am and parked the truck in just the right spot. I locked the doors and crawled into the back pulling the sliding door almost closed so I had a great view of the apartment and set up my gear. After a quick radio check with my guy's in the chase vehicles it was sit, watch and wait. About 10:00 am our target made his first appearance. He came out in his pajamas and just stood around looking while he smoked a cigarette and then disappeared back inside. He did this pretty much all day about every hour as if he was looking for something or someone.

We ran this surveillance for a total of five day's and he never once paid any attention to the truck. I however documented everything he did including vandalizing a neighbors car. With what we got there we also had enough to prove he was lying about his injuries. My ice box truck had become a pretty comfy home away from home for me and the ice worked great. During the day I would sit on the ice and be kept cool and in the evenings I would sit in my lounge chair. On the last night of the surveillance I had a pizza delivered to the truck to celebrate and my two guys joined me in the truck for dinner that night. You should have seen the look on the face of the delivery guy.

Who needs a car alarm

I received an insurance fraud case from one of my regular client's on a guy who was an electrician by trade and was alleged to be in some type of singing group. His first day on the job, he claimed he fell and injured his back and was suing for a substantial amount. Pretty much typical of most workers comp cases, but sometimes things still get interesting.

My subject lived in an apartment complex in northwest Atlanta, which unfortunately is not a real nice place. It's pretty much government housing and old industrial areas and is not the kind of place you would want to be stranded in at night. Even during the day open drug sales and prostitution are obvious and the occasional gun shots are heard.

I have found the best way to handle a situation like this is to get on location really early and find a place to park, then get in the back of the van and close the curtains. It is best to stay completely out of sight in these areas, because they are highly suspicious of strangers, especially when they are the wrong color.

So I get to the apartment complex real early and found my perfect spot. I then get in the back and close all the curtains and wait on my target to show his face. The morning passes quietly as resident's go about their daily lives, no one pays any attention to the van. As the day goes on it starts to get a little warm in the van so I decided to open my sliding side windows a little to let some fresh air in.

Later on in the day my guy finally shows his face and proceeds to work on his car in the parking lot. My target spent so much time under the hood of his car, it made my back hurt. Looks like he's doing a lot better now and I am video taping every second of it.

As I'm sitting there videoing my guy I hear someone walk up to my vehicle and what sounded like some one is trying to open the side door of my van. The next thing I notice is I see a shadow of a hand thru the curtain reaching in and sliding the window further open. I quietly turn my body fully around to face the sliding door and see an arm reach down to find the interior lock mechanism to unlock the door.

I pulled my arm back and brutally punched the guys hand as hard as I could, trapping his arm against the door. I must have scared the hell out of the guy because he started screaming like a little girl. He finally freed himself and ran off. I never even saw his face.

Who should I shoot first

Back in the early 80's when I was first starting out I used to serve a lot of legal documents to various individuals. I had gotten in with several large law firms and would get five or six a week and it was kinda fun to do and I would make a game of it and see how fast I could get it done. Not very exciting usually, but hey it pays the bills.

It was a Friday and I went by one of the law firms and picked up a few suits to serve. As I looked thru the documents I noticed the address on one and immediately recognized it. It was in the roughest neighborhood in Atlanta. The place is called Tech Wood homes and is a very dangerous place. There is a shooting there almost every night and drug dealers and prostitutes are every where.

I went out there the following Saturday afternoon hoping to get lucky and serve the guy quick. As luck would have it, once there find out that most of the street signs and building numbers were missing. I've been told by local law enforcement, that the bad guys take them down to slow their response. So I start trying to figure out where I am and exactly where my target resides. The only way to do that is start asking for directions from the locals.

After speaking with several people who were of no use at all, I finally got some directions from this very nice elderly lady. I went on my way to my targets apartment and knocked on the door. After a few minutes my guy comes to the door and I get him served. Wow, that was a lot easier than I thought.

When I walked down the stairs and into the foyer, I see a large group of African American persons standing outside. As soon as I walked out the door, they started hurling insults and wanting to know what the F--- I wanted. I tried to talk with them, however it just agitated them even more and they closed in and started making threats and acting very aggressively. A big guy, well over six feet tall, walked real close and said "no one will find your body m----- F----- when we get thru". I looked him dead in the eye and asked him if he was in charge around there and he just smiled and laughed an evil laugh.

I immediately reached into my waist band and pulled out my big ugly looking Smith & Wesson model 13, 357 magnum six shooter and stuck it in his face. I then asked him "who do I shoot first", cause I'm not dying here alone, I'm taking at least six of you with me. My new found friend suddenly started sweating profusely and had a complete change in attitude. Seems they were just kidding, all a simple misunderstanding. The crowd parted and I kept my eyes and weapon on them, got in my van and got the hell out of there.

The following Monday I went to my local gun shop and bought a Smith & Wesson model 669 capable of holding 17 rounds, just in case that happened again.

The not so covert camera installation

A couple of years ago I received a referral on a domestic situation. Our client was the wife of a fairly well to do physician. She told us that over the previous six months her husband had grown distant and was starting to verbally abuse her when they were home alone. She said he was always careful in public and around the kids, but behind closed doors it was another story and she wanted evidence. I told her video was the way to go.

We met at her house when no one else was home and she showed us around. I came up with a plan to place a covert video camera in the living room area to cover not only the living room, but the dining area as well. A second camera would be placed in the dressing area of their bedroom on the second floor where he has gone off on her several times previously, out of ear shot of the kids.

I decided to use a high end 900mz transmitter and receiver to reliably transmit the audio/video from the living room downstairs to the recording equipment concealed in a spare bedroom upstairs. The dressing room camera would be hard wired and concealed through the attic to the spare bedroom. We set up a day the following week when no one would be home to install the equipment.

We got to our clients house just after every one left so we would have time to work out any kinks we may run into during the install. I got started down stairs concealing the living room camera and transmitter in a cabinet and sent my number two guy, bulldog up stairs to start on the dressing room camera installation. The living room camera and transmitter went as planned and I went up to set up the recording equipment in the upstairs spare bedroom.

The recording equipment set up and tested out great; we had a strong signal from the camera downstairs and were almost done. Bulldog was having a problem getting the cable from the dressing room camera into the wall of the spare bedroom. The wall was built off set so he couldn't get it thru, so I went up in the attic with him to try and figure it out. After a little period of looking, drilling and cursing several times, we finally hit the jack pot and got it fed thru to the spare bedroom wall. We came back down from the attic and I finished connecting and checking the equipment, everything was good.

I sent bulldog back up into the attic to be sure the cable was well hidden and to retrieve our tools. The pull down attic stairs was in the bathroom adjacent to the spare bedroom and I watched bulldog go up the stairs out of sight. A few seconds later I hear a loud thud and his foot come thru the bathroom ceiling. He immediately starts cussing and pulls his foot back into the attic. I of course am yelling at him and asking him what the hell are you doing! A few seconds after that, we hear a huge crash and his ass comes thru the spare bedroom ceiling raining sheetrock and insulation everywhere. He comes to a rest hanging from a rafter with the camera cable around his foot. I yell at him to stay put until I freed up the cable and he then dropped to the ground. He got up with this blank look on his face, dusted himself off and said two things, first my ankle gave out and second I can fix it, then headed for his truck.

Within an hour he was back with building materials and a helper. See bulldog has his own repair company on the side, so he knew what to do and didn't waste any time.

The hard part was calling our client and telling her what happened. Thankfully she was really nice and understanding. She came up with a cover story for her husband, that entailed her going up to the attic to retrieve her sewing machine and she lost her balance and it went thru the ceiling. Surprisingly enough he bought the story. It just goes to show you no matter what, anything can happen.

Sorry, I didn't know it was you

In the late 90's I was contacted by an international high end electronics manufacture, which had some serious concerns about security at their metro Atlanta facility. I met the facility manager off premises and he informed me that they have had several highly restricted items disappear from inventory over the last two months. There were only a handful of employees who had access to the area and worked together, so it was likely one of them.

The facility manager informed me that there was an entry level position open in that department that they had been trying to fill. My advice was of course to put an undercover agent in that position to gather intelligence on that group of employees. We then set up a mock interview for my undercover agent to come in and get "hired".

My undercover agent, I called him "what a guy", started the following Monday. It didn't take "what a guy" more than a couple of weeks to get every one very comfortable with him and become one of the "guys". This group of employees was more of a party club there at work. They routinely drank and smoked pot at work and broke almost every rule in the employee handbook.

While reading over "what a guys" undercover reports I noticed a familiar name, the same as one of my old high school buddies, but surely it wasn't him I thought. I contacted my undercover agent and asked him for a physical description of the familiar name and sure enough it sounded like my old buddy. The next time "what a guy" and I met in person I showed him an old photograph of my buddy and sure enough it was him. I felt bad for him because we were getting ready to cook his goose so to speak, but ultimately I wasn't responsible for his actions.

The last day "what a guy" showed up for work everybody looked at him funny and didn't speak to him when he walked thru the door as normal. The facility manager quickly whisked him into his office. Turns out the facility manager had absent mindedly left a copy of the undercover reports out on his desk and the party club saw them, talk about stupid. Needless to say "what a guy" was out of there. My old buddy hasn't spoken to me since.

Babysitting 4.5 million back to Atlanta

In preparation for the up coming 1996 Olympic Games in Atlanta, one of my corporate security clients contacted me about a top secret operation they needed my help with. Being a major corporate sponsor they were responsible for providing secure transportation for 4.5 million dollars worth of Olympic Games tickets from a secure printing facility in Fort Smith, Arkansas to their corporate headquarters in Atlanta.

We devised a basic plan and began mapping out all the details. We carefully planned separate routes of travel both their and back to confuse any one that might want to get their hands on them. We also established a schedule for check in calls, progress reports and back up alternate routes in case of an emergency and this is how we did it.

I went to a van rental company out of Atlanta and rented a plain non-descript white Chevrolet work van and took it to my house. I then went to my local hardware store and purchased two, three foot links of beefy chain and two large master locks. I used the chains and locks to secure the side and rear doors of the van from the inside. I then taped over the rear windows with black tape and hung a curtain just to the rear of the front seats so no one would be able to peer into the vehicle and see the contents. I then furnished the van with an air mattress, large cooler, bullet proof vests, a twelve gauge riot shotgun, pee jug, fake magnets, drive out tag and snacks.

I left out of Atlanta early the next morning making my way to Little Rock, Arkansas. I rolled into town late that evening and got a hotel for the night. Early the next morning I drove to the Little Rock airport and picked up my corporate security contact and we headed for Fort Smith.

When we were getting close to Fort Smith I exited the highway and found an isolated area. We took the tag off the van and put on a drive out tag and the fake magnetic signs. We then proceeded on our way. We went straight to the secure printing facility and got loaded up. I re-secured the chains and we were set. They rolled open the steel security doors of the facility and we were off and running. Back out of town in a secure area I ditched the signs and put the tag back on.

I settled in and began the long trip back, my corporate security contact made himself comfortable in the passengers seat and we chit chatted for awhile until he fell asleep. I drove thru the day and night, only stopping for fuel and a drive thru and approached Atlanta early the following morning.

When we got close to the corporate headquarters, we picked up a second corporate security guy and I dressed them both in the bullet proof vests. We were in the home stretch and everything went like clock work. We pulled into the heavily secured parking facility and parked. The head of their corporate security department was there waiting on us and had the tickets taken up stairs. I escorted them all the way to their corporate vault and watched as they were sealed inside. I then went straight home and passed out for a few hours.

Surviving South Georgia

Back in the mid 80's I was working a fraud case in Sylvester, Georgia. Running days of surveillance down there in the dog days of summer was very draining; with all the heat and humidity all you want to find is a decent hotel room with ice cold air conditioning. After some good food and a shower you feel human again.

It was Friday and I was going home the following day after a very successful trip and I decided to go out and celebrate. I knew of a great dance club in nearby Albany and decided to go there and have some fun.

I got to the club about 9:00pm and it was already packed. I cruised by the bar and got a beer and found a spot with a good view of the dance floor. After a while I made eye contact with this gorgeous brunette and before long we were laughing, dancing and having a great time. She was a very sweet girl a real Georgia peach and was going to school to be a nurse. We hit it off really well because of my previous experience in the medical profession. Later on that night her ex-boyfriend and some of his buddies showed up and he wasn't very friendly, he just stood around staring at us. As the night went on we basically ignored them and enjoyed our evening.

I headed to the men's room to get rid of some used beer and I saw the ex head my way. When he entered the restroom he started running his mouth, so I did what came naturally and slammed his ass against the wall and explained to him that I was not to be messed with. It just so happened that the manager of the club was in the restroom at the time and threw him out.

At closing time we exchanged numbers and I walked her to her car and said good night. On the way to my vehicle I saw the ex and some of his buddies in a pick-up truck at the other end of the lot so I immediately kept a close eye on them. I got in my vehicle and headed out and watched them pull out some distance behind me. They trailed along until we got well out of town on Hwy 82.

It was after 2:00 in the morning and the highway was deserted. After a few miles they started speeding up. They came up along side me and started throwing beer bottles. The driver then started trying to run me off the road and I got real pissed off. I was pissed, but not stupid; I didn't think it would be a good idea to stop and duke it out with the four of them.

I learned early on in this profession that you better be well armed, because out there you are on your own. I reached behind my seat and grabbed my AR-15 and put a round in the chamber. I then rolled down my window and rested the barrel across my left arm and waited. The driver came up on me again and swerved toward me. I raised my weapon and cut loose with a 10 round burst into the front of the truck and it went spinning to a stop in the median. I hauled ass back to my hotel and cleaned the spent brass out of the vehicle. I checked the morning news, but nothing was said about the incident. I bet they never try that again.

Damn, that's got to suck

Years ago, I did a lot of work for an international company that had a large facility in Carrollton, Georgia. The city is a quaint small college town in the heart of Carroll County and is surrounded by mostly farm land and forestlands. This sometimes makes surveillance very difficult, especially in the more isolated areas.

My client contacted me regarding an older individual who alleged to have had a bizarre accident in there facility several years ago when he was employed there. He alleged that while working on a piece of machinery the hammer he was using bounced back and struck him in the head. He stated that he was momentarily knocked out and now can't remember stuff; his speech was affected and was barely able to walk.

Unfortunately, this guy lived out in the sticks on the bank of the Tallapoosa River. We tried various means to surveil him but were not getting a lot of activity out of him. We really couldn't get close enough to him, how ever we could hear him doing things and working on something that was out of our view. This was a large case and our client asked us to continue our efforts.

After several more boring days we finally caught him leaving his property one day around noon. He proceeded west towards the town of Bowdon, Georgia in his pick-up truck. When he got to town he stopped at the hardware store that is where he started a two and a half hour shopping spree all over town. He seemed to feel quite comfortable away from Carrollton were he is fairly well known.

I was able to document him walking, talking, laughing and of course driving thru the entire shopping trip. If he had any sort of neurological problem he sure didn't act like it. When he finished shopping he headed out of town towards Alabama, not Carrolton. I just stayed with him believing he was probably headed for his rumored girlfriend's house.

We drove well into Alabama before he finally turned off on a dirt road. I continued past to avoid being obvious and turned around. I gave it a few seconds and then proceeded down the road trailing the dust trail from his vehicle. After what seemed like ten miles the dust trail just disappeared in an area that there were four different ways he could of went.

I picked one road and hauled ass, hoping to catch up with him. I drove that road to the end with no sign of my guy, so I turned around and hauled ass back to try another road. I picked a second road and took off down it, but no sign of him that way either. I hit the third road flying, knowing my chances of finding were growing less with every second that passed. I came to a sudden sharp right hand curve and tried to slow down, but I was going too fast and slid thru the turn. I met up with my guy coming from the other direction in the apex of the turn. He swerved hard right and ran off the road into a swampy area and pegged a tree. I decided I got enough on him already that day and it was time I disappeared. I still wonder how long it took him to get out of there.

The crazy client

Having been in this business all these years I have dealt with all types of people. People like you and me come from all walks of life and you can't judge any one by their status in the community, their financial status or lack there of. I have met some wonderful people of meager means and plenty of well off assholes. Sometimes you come in contact with someone you think is normal, however they turn out to be whacked out beyond belief. This case turned out to be one of the latter.

One of my corporate security clients was contacted by a well to do lady whom needed to have her residence sweeped for listening devises. She relayed to him she was embroiled in some "big" things and was afraid her privacy had been compromised. I informed him of my schedule and when I would be available to do a countermeasures sweep. A week or so went by and my client contacted me to arrange for us to meet the lady at her house to conduct the sweep.

We arrived at the sprawling residence in a very upscale Atlanta neighborhood and made our way to the front door. After a few minutes our lady answered the door and let us in. She had been previously warned not to speak about what we were doing until I completed the search, so if there was something found the person on the listening end wouldn't know. She seemed to be a very educated, articulate lady and everything seemed normal.

I started my methodical electronic search of the residence downstairs and worked my way up thru to the top floor. It is a slow painstakingly thorough process to make sure every area is properly searched. By utilizing a wide band receiver you hunt for any type of electronic signals that are being emitted from anything in the residence. Not many people know this, but we are being bombarded with radio signals constantly and you have to weed thru those signals to find any signal being generated on the premises. Then you move on to the second phase of the countermeasures search which is the physical search. You must inspect any and all areas that something could be placed or hidden in. You must look for everything from voice activated records to actual bugs. Once that has been completed you move on to the final phase where you test and analyze all telephone lines coming into the residence.

We got finished up and I packed my gear. I went down to speak to our lady and let her know the house was all clear. She seemed in utter disbelief that nothing was found and insisted that there must be something in the house. She said the kind of information that had "gotten out", could only have come from within the house. I pressed her to be more specific so I would have some idea what she was talking about. Reluctantly she began to explain what she thought was going on. She stated that a Hollywood comedian who was popular on television was surveilling her in her house for his comedy routine material and even called her one night to taunt her with it. I held my tongue got my check and politely left. She didn't need a Detective, she needed a shrink.

You're not my uncle

Thru the years I have learned the particular difficulties in working in some areas. For instance I know that any case that has to be worked in the mountains is going to provide many challenges to a successful surveillance operation. Then you combine that with not having an exact address for your target and it gets exponentially more difficult.

I received a potential insurance fraud assignment on a male individual who allegedly recently moved to a retirement community in the North Georgia Mountains. He was making all sorts of claims about various injuries and ailments from a small traffic accident that were frankly ridiculous. It was a very primitive development in the mountains where the residences were well secluded and not numbered. The community had a general store at the entrance and a mail station where the resident's retrieve their mail.

All I had to go on was sketchy partial directions and a description of my targets vehicle and that was all. I slipped thru the gate and started following the directions that I had been given by our client. It soon became apparent that the directions weren't even close to being accurate, so I started riding the roads searching for the targets vehicle. The development was huge and I spent hours looking and hunting trying to pin down exactly where he was living.

After that didn't produce any positive results I tried asking any one I could find out and about if they knew him or who might. Sometimes you have to just do things the old fashioned way. No fancy this or that just patience and persistence and get out there and beat the bush's so to speak. Sometimes that last little thing you do or think of will finally give you success.

Finally, one nice gentleman suggested that I speak to the man that runs the general store back down the mountain at the entrance. I headed on my way back down the mountain. The ride seemed like it took for ever to get back down to the store, my brakes were actually smoking when I finally stopped, that's how steep the roads were.

I entered the store and waited my turn as the man behind the counter waited on customers. When it was my turn I stepped up to the counter and asked him if he knew where my target lived. He looked at me and said, well that's me. Out of thin air I blurted out, you're not my uncle! I told him I was looking for my long lost uncle who was supposed to be living somewhere in the area.

When I walked out the door of the store I then noticed his vehicle parked outside. I'm pretty sure he bought the story, because I was able to get everything I needed on him.

It's a miracle!

I received a call from one our large medical malpractice insurers on a file down in South Georgia. The case involved a thirty five year old woman who had brain surgery after a car accident. She claimed that the surgeon botched the surgery and she was now terribly impaired. Her attorney claimed that she was now pretty much a vegetable and had to be led around by her hand. He further alleged that she now lives at home with her parents who have to provide twenty four hour care for her.

It was a large case worth millions and they were coming up on the trial date. They wanted to see if she was in as bad of shape as they were making it sound. Unfortunately, they waited until they were fast approaching the trial date before calling me. I have found that the closer they are to a trial date an untruthful claimant will be more conscience and careful about what they do to protect their big payoff.

The parents lived in the lazy South Georgia town of Vidalia. It's always been a neat little town fully of old south charm. I located the parent's house and found the set up was terrible. The residence was on a small single track dirt lane in a lower income area. Over the next few days I was able to get video of the person I believed to be my target. She would periodically exit the residence to smoke a cigarette, but the view was partially obscured by a tree. She definitely fit the description though so I tried to get anything I could on her.

After two trips down there it was trial time. My client managed to settle the case at the very last minute for a few million less than the demand. He didn't want to have to try it in front of a jury, because it could cost them a lot more.

Exactly one month after they settled the case, my client contacted me and asks me to reopen the file. Seems like the video I did get was bothering he and I both. First trip down the place looked deserted, except for the parent's car. Something wasn't right, because her kids were no where around.

Before my next trip down I ran background research on her again, but nothing was showing up new. My gut told me she was no longer there, but where is she. The next trip down I decided to do some in depth research at the county courthouse, but still nothing new. On my way out I decided to check the voter registration office just so I left no stone unturned. Eureka! She had just registered to vote the previous week at a new address in the neighboring town of Lyons.

Seems like she had made a miraculous recovery, she now had a new house with an in ground pool, two new SUV's and she is out and about everywhere shopping, driving and dining out. She did real well driving and yakking on her cell phone and was now able to run around the yard playing with her kids and dog. She also gave some killer parties. Well, that was before she was arrested and prosecuted for felony insurance fraud.

I should have brought a bigger gun

Back when I was first starting out in this business I went to work as an undercover agent for a large established Atlanta P.I. firm. I worked numerous assignments for this firm, mostly in manufacturing or warehouse type of settings. I would work these assignments for various purposes, mostly to gather intelligence on suspected drug use by employees, theft of company property and other violations of various company policies.

I had just finished a successful undercover operation at a manufacturing facility in Norcross, Georgia and was enjoying a few days off. My phone rang and it was my handler from the P.I. firm. He had a position he wanted to put me in at a specialized automotive manufacturing facility in Duluth, Georgia. They were experiencing thefts of a very expensive alloy used in the manufacturing process and the losses were in the tens of thousands and growing.

I was scheduled for my "interview" the following Monday, so I could get hired. Everything went as planned and I started the process of settling in and getting the vibe of the place. I was placed on the second shift after the second week which put me in a position to work with the mostly unsupervised second shift. The atmosphere was much more relaxed and everybody was friendly.

After a few weeks on the second shift I got to know the guys on the crew fairly well. None of them even hinted about any wrong doings and were really a pretty conscientious bunch. They for the most part came in and did a good job and were there every day. A few more weeks go by and everything is still the same. My undercover reports became boring and redundant because there was nothing going on. Every shift was the same, we clocked in worked and then clock out and go home with the shift supervisor waiting for every one to leave before he locked up for the night.

One day it finally dawned on me that the only person that could get away with the thefts, would be some one who had access to the entire facility alone without an audience. That left only one person, the shift supervisor. He was a decorated Vietnam Vet and a twenty year employee. He didn't seem like the type, but I had to check it out.

On my next shift everything was as usual. When the whistle blew we clocked out and headed for the wash room to get all the black filth off of our hands. I purposely stood around talking while the guys cleaned up. When they were about thru I started cleaning up and the last one left as they said goodbye. I finished up and snuck out of the washroom and found a good hiding place to observe the shift supervisor. Moments later he briskly walked thru and closed one of the two roll up doors and disappeared. A minute later he backed his conversion van into the open door. He exited the vehicle and walked out of view after opening the back door. He came back into view on an electric forklift with a roll of metal on it and loaded it in the van. I confronted him when he came back and he went nuts, he reached in the van and retrieved a shotgun. I pulled out my puny Smith & Wesson 32cal and tried to be intimidating. That apparently didn't work, because he sent a round of buck shot my way peppering my arm and leg. I fired two rounds in his direction to keep his head down and quickly get the hell out of there as fast as possible. I was way out gunned and I wasn't getting paid that much. I bolted out of the open door and hauled ass along the chain link fence towards the guard shack and parking lot, keeping an eye out for asshole as I went. I don't know who called them I assumed the guards, but as I reached the gate, two local P.D. units arrived on scene. I was very glad to see them. I quickly briefed them on the situation and they took over from there.

Apparently this guy was so well known and respected there that the guards never checked his vehicle even though he always parked inside the fence to the rear of the facility. Now he faced felony theft charges, assault with a deadly weapon and various other charges. Not to mention he lost his job and retirement.

Bulldog has a strange sense of humor

One of our insurance clients contacted us on a file involving a gentleman whom allegedly was injured on his job and could no longer work. He alleged a back and neck injury and was making a substantial claim for permanent disability.

He had a live in girlfriend who was privy to what was going on with his claim and that he was looking forward to a sizeable settlement. Unfortunately for him, she caught him messing around with another woman and she decided to get even. She called the claims handler and proceeded to give her a detail list of his usual activities including his workout schedule. Turns out he had a regular workout schedule at one of the big name gyms in his area. This was going to be easy.

I assigned bulldog to the file and set him up with a pager cam. The first day of surveillance was totally unfruitful; it seems that the only time someone deviates from their routine is when you're counting on them to stay on schedule. The second day out he was right on schedule and headed for the gym. Bulldog let him go in first and then went in and got a day pass.

He located our target and worked out close by to him with the camera trained on the target the entire time. The guy that was claiming complete and total disability was doing heavy squats, leg presses and dead lifts the entire time. He trained with great intensity and concentration, not paying attention to anything, but his training. The guy wasn't a health nut, he was a power lifter.

After the workout, bulldog followed him into the locker room. Bulldog then proceeds to shoot about twenty minutes worth of video of a bunch of fat hairy guys walking around naked in the shower area, while he changed cloths. When I saw the tape I laughed my ass off and it was a real big hit around my client's office.

I really hated having to do it

We had made numerous trips out to Chilton, Alabama on a multi million dollar fraud case for one of my regular clients. The location was isolated on a hill, off a busy county road and extremely difficult to surveil. I had spent a lot of time living in the woods across the highway from my targets property and was having limited success. I really wanted to get to the truth on this case. There were so many things going on up on that hill. There was a regular flow of people going up to the target's residence out of view, staying various lengths of time then departing. Unfortunately, from my position, I could not see much of anything.

The best approach was to covertly infiltrate the forest area surrounding his property and surveil his property and residence from the rear. I knew from previous aerial recon, that the targets property had been completely cleared out to the property line with a bulldozer. To the rear of his property was all dense forest and was ideal for covert surveillance ops. There was however one huge problem, actually two huge problems in the form of Rottweiler's. My target had two huge ones and they literally patrolled the entire area. Having already had an encounter with them previously, I knew it was a risky venture.

I devised a plan to attempt to pull off covert ops from the rear of his property. I would insert well away from the target area and circumnavigate around in the forest and make a careful approach from the rear. I would move in just close enough to see the target and hide there. To hopefully ward off any contact with the dogs, I would sprinkle ground red pepper in a large circle around me to throw off their sense of smell. If I did encounter the dog's I would carry a suppressed Ruger Mark I and an Olympic OA-98 pistol.

The first time in I took bulldog with me; actually he made me take him with me because he didn't want me to go it alone. He's like my adopted brother and watch's out for me. I spent several weeks prior to the op teaching him proper patrol techniques and sniper skills, so he wouldn't get us in trouble. We had some success that trip and were able to get in and out with no problem. We saw the dogs several times, but they never knew we were there.

A few weeks later I would do my second solo surveillance op up on that hill. I started out as usual early in the morning when the shadows are long and it was cool. I carefully made my way on my first leg of the trip, going due north to a fire road down hill from the target area. I arrived at the fire road and peered out of the brush and the coast looked clear. As I stepped out in the open one of the rottweiler's appeared at the crest of the hill on the road. He immediately started barking viciously and charging down the hill. I dropped to one knee and steadied my suppressed Mark I and started firing. I pumped seven rounds into that animal and it kept charging. The last round dropped him dead, literally at my feet. It took me three and half hours to drag that huge dog into the woods far enough to bury him where he wouldn't be found. I hated having to do it, but it was him or me.

At least they'll know what happened

Back in the mid eighties I did a lot of surveillance cases in rural South Georgia. We had several insurance clients that wrote workers compensation policies to large agriculture and manufacturing operations in the region. Performing surveillance in a rural setting has its own unique set of challenges. In many areas there are vast open flat fields everywhere you look and absolutely no place to hide.

I received one of these workers comp files in an area near Douglas, Georgia. The target resided on one of those long straight flat rural roads near an intersection of another long straight flat road. The area was dotted with the occasional house or mobile home and the rest of the area was covered by vast open fields. In this situation you have few options; with absolutely no place to hide you literally have to do the old "hide in plain sight" routine.

What I mean by that is you have to come up with a plausible benign reason for lingering in the area, without giving away your real mission at hand. I would use bogus magnet vehicle signs and related props to appear as a surveyor, telecommunication or utility inspector so I could belay suspicions of local residents and especially my target. It amazed me on many occasions how most people will believe just about anything when you have a good story and signs.

After doing several ride by's of the target's residence the previous evening, I assumed the initial surveillance position very early in the morning before sunrise. This initial position was the furthest distance away from the target residence that I could still see the house. My modus operandi was to watch initially for the subject to depart the area in the morning and initiate mobile surveillance. If the target did not leave during the morning hours, then I would slowly "work" my way closer to the target and see if I could pick up on any activity at the residence.

The first day of surveillance was absolutely boringly quiet. I would have the occasional passer by and that was it. There were two vehicles parked at the target residence, but no one came or went not even to check the mail. I was feeling pretty comfortable with the set up so I decided to do the same routine the following day, just from a different direction.

I got out the next morning just as I did the first day and assumed my initial surveillance position. After a few hours went by I started my slow approach of the target residence. I had gotten within two hundred yards of the targets residence when low and behold out he came and started working on his truck. He was doing all sorts of things he claimed he couldn't do. As I was pretending to check a nearby utility box my camera in the van was recording his every move. The target moved the truck to another area of the yard under a large Oak tree. I returned to the van quickly so I could reposition my camera. As I peered thru the view finder I observed the target leaning across the hood of the truck and taking aim directly at me with a scoped high powered rifle. I kept shooting video tape just hoping he wouldn't pull the trigger. He didn't.

Air America's final revenge

Back in the mid 80's I was contacted by an old associate of mine from days gone by who had a problem. He was a retired Air America pilot that used to fly covert missions in Southeast Asia. After coming home he got a commercial pilots job and was based in Atlanta. He then met and fell in love with a CPA he had met and they were married. A few years go by and she starts to become detached and distant and he knew something was wrong.

He tried talking with her to no avail and she would always claim it was just that she was overwhelmed at work. They had two beautiful young children and he felt very strongly about doing the right thing for the kids so he just went on as usual. As time went on things got worse between the two of them. He very much wanted to work things out, however she was still keeping up the charade.

He finally started snooping around himself and even started taping all conversations on the home phone. After a period of time passed he realized that she was being very careful and was covering her tracks. He knew she was up to something, but he couldn't find any evidence. It then dawned on him that she could be concealing evidence in her office, which was off limits to him.

Her office was located in an office complex not to far from where they lived. She and one employee were in sole possession of the keys to the office and she never let them out of her sight. He had previously looked for them while she was tied up with family visiting, however he couldn't find them to make a copy. This only fueled his suspicion that there was something at the office she didn't want him to see.

That's where I come in; he wanted me to pick the lock so he could go in and search the office. He had been there for me in a time of need so I felt obligated to help him out. I got the address from him so I could check the location out and see what I had to work with. After checking out the office park I realized that they had a patrolling guard service that drove thru on the hour and half hour. And they were usually right on time; the complex was adjacent to a wooded area that would provide cover to get to her particular office. All we had to do was wait till the security guard made his rounds and we were good to go.

The night we conducted the op, it was pouring down rain. I liked this because it provided an additional layer of cover. We got into position and waited on the security guard. He showed up right on time and when he left we moved in. I inserted my tension tool into the lock and began to rake the lock with my pick and the damn thing just broke. We retreated back to the van to retrieve another pick. We get back into position to await the security guard to make his rounds. As soon as he did we moved in again and I started on the lock. Sixty seconds later the lock was defeated and he was in, we shook hands and I left. He told me later he found everything he needed in her date book. My debt was now paid in full.

Splat, there goes that case

One of my long time clients contacted me regarding what he believed was a fraudulent workers compensation claim. The individual involved worked in their Carrollton, Georgia facility in the warehouse area and claimed to have slipped and fell on a wet floor. He now alleged that he suffered a completely debilitating back injury with migraine headaches and was now bedridden.

As luck would have it, he resided in a very remote area just over the state line in Alabama. He lived off a single track dirt road and the residence was completely obscured from view. He owned the five acres where his house was located and it was built in the center of the property. In a situation like this a covert surveillance op was not feasible, because you would have to trespass on his property to surveil him. The only other choice was to set up on the most likely route of departure and wait. My client had provided me with his vehicle description so I knew what he would be driving.

I started the first day of surveillance bright and early in the morning. I went thru the day and saw only two vehicles travel the road, neither being my subject's. Time passed fairly quickly though it was a very mild day and I had a shady spot to sit. Performing surveillance in the summer time can be extremely punishing with the heat and humidity down in the south, temperatures can easily reach one hundred twenty degrees inside a vehicle. If you plan on surviving it you better take plenty of cold water to keep yourself hydrated and just sweat it out.

The second, third and fourth days of surveillance played out not to different than the first, very little traffic passing by and absolutely no sign of my target. Unfortunately in the real world this happens. Some people are very inactive by nature and can be quite the home body, only leaving their residence when they have to. I contacted my client with my findings or lack there of and suggested we terminated the surveillance efforts for the time being. It is very difficult to justify sitting out there day after day and not get any results. My client asked me to go out one more day on it and I reluctantly agreed. I hate boring cases but you have to accommodate your client's wishes.

I decided to work the last day on the file the following Saturday. Nothing happened on the previous week day surveillances so I felt it was my best last shot at it. I set up as usual and settled in for another boring day. Around about ten O'clock here comes my targets vehicle. I hunkered down and he passed me and just sat there and watched him drive around a turn and go out of sight. I waited a few seconds before I started after him and moved out slowly. I stayed back as far as I could without loosing him as he made his way to a main road. When he hit the main highway he headed west and I carefully slid in behind him. A few miles down the road he pulled off on the shoulder of the road. At first I thought he made me, but as I passed by him I realized he had a flat tire. I went down about a quarter of a mile and turned around. I pulled onto the shoulder of the road about two hundred yards away from where he stopped to video him changing his tire. When he stepped out of his truck, he was immediately struck by an on coming semi truck. He was killed instantly, and that was the end of that case.

There's always one asshole sheriff

Back in the eighties, I received a particular assignment on a suspected fraud case down in Grady County in extreme South Georgia. My client only had very sketchy information on the individual in question and only had an old address near the city of Cairo. He was believed to still be in the same area, but his exact place of residence was not known. In those days there were very few sources of information that you could use to attempt to locate somebody. You could try pretext telephone calls to old neighbors, courthouse research in the county they resided and local law enforcement contacts to attempt to ferret some one out. The last option is to make personal contact with any one and everyone who might know your target.

I knew before I left out on the case that it was probably going to be a real pain in the ass. I figured at best I had a fifty percent chance of even locating the guy, much less be able to surveil him. Not to be judgmental, but some places in South Georgia are real back woods and you never know how they will react to a stranger in town looking for a local. Sometimes you just have to roll the dice and see what happens.

I headed out on the long trip down to Cairo early in the morning so I could get there in plenty enough time to do preliminary research at the local public library before heading to the county courthouse. In those days we would use the Haynes directory for the local area to identify neighbors and their telephone numbers of your targets old known addresses. I pulled a half dozen or so old neighbors telephone numbers that I would use later on to try and develop information on my target.

I then proceeded to the courthouse to do my research of all available records that might point me in the right direction. Some of those records are deeds, mortgages, financing statements, voter registration, traffic, magistrate, state and superior court records. No new information was showing up anywhere on my target.

My next step was to physically go out to his last known address and poke around. When I got there I noted several vehicles there at the time. I wrote down all the tag numbers and then decided to approach the residence under a pretext, however no pertinent information was revealed.

The next step was to contact the county sheriff's office and find out what they may know about my target. When I walked into the sheriff's office I got a funny feeling right off the bat. I showed my credentials and told them what I was trying to do. I was asked to wait a moment and was then escorted to the sheriff's personal office. He was your stereotypical fat, redneck asshole. He started out by telling me I didn't look like an investigator and it went down hill from there. The more he flapped his ignorant gums the more pissed off I got. I finally said screw it and left without any cooperation at all. As I drove towards the county line I was boiling, thinking about what a jackass the guy was. I stopped at a pay phone and called the sheriff's office and got the prick on the phone. I called that ass wipe every name in the book and told him exactly what I thought of him. I then slammed down the phone and got the hell out of his county.

I wish I hadn't done that

It was the middle of another record breaking hot summer in Georgia. A rush case was called in on a Thursday and my client needed it worked over the coming weekend, the case was going to trial in the very near future and it had been accidentally over looked and they wanted to get surveillance done before it was too late. I cancelled my weekend plans and started my preparations for the trip.

I had a new investigator in training at the time and I asked him if he wanted to go with me and he eagerly said yes. I nicked named the guy captain K for certain reasons I won't go into, but it's a funny story itself. He was a great guy with tremendous potential and drive, as he later went on to work with the Georgia Bureau of Investigation and the U.S. Drug Enforcement Administration.

Captain K arrived at my house very early Friday morning and we headed out to Macon where the case was located. We made great time on the drive down and were on location before dawn. We found a suitable surveillance position and settled in to watch for our target. About ten that morning our target exited his residence and we were able to shoot some video tape on him as he took out the trash and picked a few pieces of garbage in the yard. No big deal really, but at least we have a good ID on him and we knew he was home.

The remainder of the day was pretty uneventful and we decided to call it a day at four p.m. and went to check into a hotel. I decided to stay at the new nicest hotel in town because they had great amenities and the best restaurant and night club in town. Hey it was the weekend and we had to work so why not treat yourself a little bit. After we checked in and cleaned up it was dinner time so we went down stairs and ate dinner. We then went upstairs for a while to relax.

About nine p.m. we went back down stairs to the club and got a table. Our waitress took our order and we began to talk. After a little while our waitress started hanging out with us and we began to cut up and make her laugh. She was a real hottie and we began to flirt and before you knew it we were starting to make out. She asked me to meet her when she got off and I of course agreed and we cruised back up to the room.

I met her at quitting time and we decided to have a few drinks, and then a few more and a few more. Before I knew it we were back at her place and going to it like rabbits. When I woke up the next morning I was still tipsy, but I had a big smile on my face. I rushed to the hotel and picked captain K up and we were off.

We got on location and set up and I was feeling rough. After a short time our target headed out and went to a flea market, where we discovered he had a booth where he sold various items. The only place to surveil from was an asphalt parking lot and it got hot quick. The temperature in the van was a good one hundred twenty degrees by noon and I was sweating liquor and trying not to puke or pass out. I thought I was going to die. We got the guy good, but I barely survived. I won't ever do that again.

The crate

I got a call from my client in Carrollton, Georgia regarding an old workers compensation claim. Seems the guy and his attorney were just dragging the case out just to build up medical expenses and the value of the case. The case had dragged on for several years and they were getting tired of the whole thing. The accident the guy was involved in was a very minor slip and there was no way he sustained the injuries he was claiming.

As is common in many cases I've worked in the area, his residence was located off a single track dirt road and was obscured from view from the road. This is a really bad set up for surveillance because there is nothing you can do but sit somewhere and hope your target leaves.

I set up early the first morning where I could just see the end of his driveway. I did so because I had no vehicle description for him so I would have to ID it if he came out. As the day went on I noted the occasional vehicle would arrive and then eventually depart his residence. I could clearly see none of these individuals matched my targets description so I'm wondering who these people are.

I broke the surveillance off mid afternoon and went to get a bite to eat. There was a sub shop in a shopping center close by so I headed over there. I got out of my vehicle and stood on the sidewalk while I finished my cigarette and started looking at the various ads posted on the community billboard. I was just about finished and saw an ad for a discounted auto repair service and noted that it was my targets ad. The ad included his name, telephone number and directions to his shop at his residence. I pocketed the ad and called it a day and began planning how to nail the guy.

This was well before the advent of micro mini cameras and all the neat gadgets we have now so I had to get creative. I came up with the idea of using a crate large enough for a person to hide in as a surveillance platform. I would place it in the back of my van and would have a perfect view of the engine area, with the hood open so we could video tape him working. I had one of my guy's to help me get it built so we could execute my plan.

Two days later we were ready to go and headed out to Carrollton mid morning. When we got in the area I stopped the van and proceeded to use a needle to put several small holes in my top radiator hose just enough to produce a noticeable leak. My guy crawled in the crate and we were off. I pulled into his driveway and drove back to his house and shop. He was a friendly sort of fellow and came out to greet me. I showed him the problem and he said he could fix it no problem, but we would have to give it some time to cool off a little. He proceeded to work on another vehicle in the meantime as we casually talked. My guy in the crate was rolling video tape the entire time. When he repaired my vehicle we got even better video of him doing all these things he claimed he couldn't do. He wound up not getting a dime for his claim.

The package and the crazy guy

I received a call from one of my corporate security clients regarding an event coming up in the near future. They were preparing for their annual stockholders meeting at their corporate offices in downtown Atlanta. The CEO would be coming in from New York to attend and they had a big security concern.

Several months prior one of their security guards became very disgruntled with the company and went berserk on the job. He shot up one of their office locations and was subsequently arrested. He made bail and got out of jail and was now constantly harassing and threatening the CEO of the company via e-mail and letter. He apparently blamed him for his perceived miss treatment. They learned that the crazy guy had actually been treated for a mental illness in the state he previously resided in so their corporate security department was quite concerned for the CEO's safety.

We sat down and laid out a plan not only to provide the CEO with a security escort for his entire stay in Atlanta, but to also put the crazy guy under twenty four hour surveillance while he was here. That way we could be prepared for the known threat and also any unknown potential threat. We had only six days to examine and evaluate the two primary locations we would be working in. We mapped everything out so we could have alternate emergency exits and entrances at the corporate offices and the hotel where the CEO would be staying. We then thoroughly checked out the residence and surrounding area of our crazy guy so we would know every street in and out of the area.

We set up surveillance on the crazy guy the day before the CEO was to arrive and ran it twenty four hours a day. We broke it up in eight hour shifts per investigator so we could be sure to stay sharp. We sure didn't want to have this guy disappear on us. The CEO arrived at the airport and our security escort team met him there and we were on the roll with the "package". We drove into the secure underground parking lot of their building and escorted the package to the boardroom. Our two teams were in constant communication by radio so we would know if the crazy guy headed our way or any other issue arose.

We went thru the first day without any hitches at all. When the meeting was done for the day we prepared to move the package to the hotel were he was staying and a reception was scheduled for later that evening. After the reception we put the package to bed and took shifts until morning

The second day we delivered the package to the boardroom and assumed our over watch positions. At about 10:30 a.m. the investigator running surveillance on the crazy guy radioed in to let me know he was on the move. The crazy guy got on I-75 heading into downtown Atlanta and my guy was right behind him. As he reached downtown I posted two members of my security team in the lobby of the building to await his potential arrival. Fortunately he continued on thru town and headed for Macon. When the day was done we put the package on a plane back to New York and we called it a day.

Oh crap, can you give me a hand

One of our insurance clients called in a case on a young guy who lived in rural central Georgia. It was a personal injury claim brought by his father. The young man was in a relatively minor auto accident and now the father was claiming his son had all sorts of injuries and could hardly get out of bed. It was during the summer time so school was out and I knew he wouldn't be on a regular schedule.

I headed out to their residence in Jackson, Georgia on a Thursday afternoon so I could get a look around the area and see what I had to work with. The set up was O.K. but by no means ideal. I had a decent place to set up and not be obvious, but you couldn't see the residence except from the road directly in front of the house.

I started the surveillance early Friday morning and got settled in. the father left for work shortly after seven a.m. and the mom headed out about an hour later. All was quiet till early afternoon when his sister left. I did periodic ride bys of the residence hoping to catch a glimpse of my target. His sister came and went several times thru out the day, but no sign on my guy. Later on that day mom and dad come home and all is quiet. My target had not shown himself at all and I knew he was either just lazy or he was being unusually careful for such a young guy. The father probably had instructed him to "play his cards right' in hopes of getting a big payoff.

I started Saturday out early and hoped the day would be more productive than the first. I absolutely hate coming home empty handed, because this business can be fickle. You can be a hero one day and a zero the next so I always want to do my best for our clients. Come mid morning mom and dad were out and about. At lunch time the daughter was visited by three of her friends, but still no sign of my guy.

At three O'clock p.m. I started to terminate the surveillance, but then decided to give it one more hour. If nothing happen by then, than I felt it was time to call it off and go home. At three thirty a full size Ford Bronco pulled into my targets driveway. It was occupied by three teenaged males and I was hoping it was my targets buddies picking him up.

Sure enough the Bronco pulled out and there were four occupants now. I followed the vehicle for quite some time before we arrived at a large softball complex on the other side of town. They met up with a group of guys and prepared to choose teams and play a game. I located a perfect spot to park where I had a great view of the field it was just in the grass at the end of the parking lot. I sat there for quite some time video taping the game. Actually my target was pretty athletic and apparently didn't have any physical problems at all. At the end of the game they got back in the Bronco and proceeded to leave. They first went in the opposite direction that we came in. I fired up the van and started after them but I went no where. It had rained heavily the previous night and unbeknownst to me I parked in a grassy mud hole and my tires just spun. About the time I get out to inspect the predicament my target and his buddies pulled up and ask if I needed a hand. They pushed me out of the mud and I was on my way. Nice kid!

Home sweet ditch

Some times it seems you just can't get a break. After a long string of very difficult cases we were assigned a fraud investigation in Stockbridge, Georgia on an older gentleman. At first I thought it would be a workable set up because I was very familiar with the area. I had worked close to that location in the past with great success and was optimistic about this one.

However, after running my initial research on the target I noted that all of his neighbor's have the same last name as his. This is never a good situation when your target is surrounded by family. Since it is very likely they all communicate on a regular basis any news will travel fast. Especially news of a strange vehicle hanging around.

My initial surveillance revealed my worst fears, the targets residence was actually a small farm complete with a sizable garden and several cattle on a narrow, curvy black top road and he was indeed surrounded by family. In a situation like this sometimes we will approach a local resident under a pretext and get permission to set up on their property. When it's all family you just don't have that option. I knew damn well he would be out working on the property, but there was absolutely no way I could think of to document it.

A couple of days later I had an idea. Since the road they lived on was a public road there was a public right of way on each side of it. If I could find a suitable place to hide with a view of my targets property in the public right of way I could use a ghillie suit to conceal myself and get what I needed on video.

The next day I rode back out to the surveillance location and began my search for a hideout. I noted a stand of brush and bamboo in a ditch in the apex of a curve in the road that would provide the three things I needed. First it would help conceal my presence, secondly it was in a good location to surveil my targets property and would be the best place to be quickly dropped off and picked up. I would use my second man to drop me off and have him hide down the street in case the target left the property.

The following Monday morning we headed out well before dawn to the surveillance location. We were on site before first light and I inserted with no problem. I quickly made myself at home in the ditch and awaited my targets appearance.

About 10:30 a.m. my target exited his house and began his day of chores on his little farm. He started with feeding the cows and chickens and then started work on his barn. He worked his ass off until about 1:00 p.m. and broke for lunch. Forty five minutes later he was back out at it, trying to get his tractor to start and hand weeding the garden. I shot three video tapes full of evidence and burned thru four batteries throughout that day. He had no clue that I was less than fifty yards away. When he finally finished I called for extraction and headed home with a big smile on my face.

Greed will do you in

I got a call from one of my friend's daughter. She was having an on going theft problem at her home. She and her husband lived in an apartment in College Park, Georgia with their child and mother in law. Her husband was of Hispanic descent and for what ever reason he was untrusting of banks. He would hide their savings in a dresser drawer in their bedroom that was not locked. Here lately they noticed some of the cash missing and couldn't figure out who was stealing it, all total twelve hundred dollars was missing. They certainly couldn't believe it was the mother in law, because she did not go anywhere or buy anything by her self.

After we sat down and talked for a little while, I suggested that we install a covert video camera in the bedroom so we could determine who the thief was. We set the installation up for a day that the mother in law was at a doctor's appointment with her son.

I met Linda at her house after her husband and mother in law left for the doctor's appointment. I set up and tested the equipment in less than an hour and all we had to do was wait. I had Linda write the serial numbers down on a dozen bait bills and put the rest of it in the bank. A week goes by and nothing happens, the bills are still there untouched.

The following Friday I got a call from Linda and the bills were missing. I went right over and pulled the surveillance tape so we could watch it. I popped it in the VCR and rewound it. Then there in living color is video of the exterminator making himself at home and getting a generous tip. We contacted the College Park Police department and provided them a copy of the tape. When they arrested them he still had a few of the marked bills in his pocket.

Now the rest of the story. At the time of this case my current number two man, bulldog was going to P.O.S.T. mandate school for certification as a law enforcement officer. This is the school that everyone who wants to become a police officer or sheriff's deputy in the State of Georgia must attend and pass.

One day they had two guest lectures come in from the College Park police department. They were there to lecture on evidence collection and surveillance techniques employed in the field. They went thru their spiel for a couple of hours and then did a question and answer session. After they finished that they set up the television to show various surveillance footage.

The first video they cued up they described as covert surveillance footage that they actually shot themselves on a theft case. They turned the video on and within sixty seconds, bulldog recognized the tape as the same one I showed him at the office two months earlier. Bulldog is one of those guys who aren't going to keep their mouth shut and proceeded to bust them out in front of the entire class. He embarrassed the hell out of both of them. He still passed the class though.

Crazy drunk lady at the VFW

Very early in my career as a P.I. I received a workers compensation claim investigation on an older lady that lived in Barnesville, Georgia. This was so long ago I had just gotten one of the first video cameras to come out on the market. It was one of those huge shoulder held cameras with the separate VHS recording deck. They both used these huge batteries that weighed about a pound each.

I headed out on my way to the surveillance location in my 1978 Chevy van early in the morning. It was still nice and cool outside and I was enjoying it while I could. It was summer time and the old love machine didn't have air conditioning. When I got on location I picked my spot and parked.

After the sun came up people started to stir in the neighborhood. People heading out to work and the joggers were out enjoying the cool morning. Later on the kids come out and start to play and everything was going well. No nosey neighbors poking around is always a good thing.

Shortly after lunch my little old lady left the house in her car. It quickly became quite apparent that either she wasn't a very good driver or she was already tipsy. It seemed we drove down and around every back road in the county before we finally arrived at the local VFW. She got out of the car and went inside.

About an hour and a half of baking in the sun in the parking lot, I see her stagger out the door with a cigarette in her mouth. She's mumbling and talking to herself as she staggered about the parking lot. She finally made her way back inside after smacking herself in the head

An hour later she's back out again and even drunker than before. Her wig is on backwards and she was carrying on a conversation with an imaginary person. She then staggers over to a car in the parking lot and starts to talk to it. She sat on the ground talking to the car for a few minutes, and then crawls back inside on her hands and knees.

She comes back out a third time barely able to stand up with a beer in her hand. Her wig is now on sideways and her shirt is about half off. She staggers over to my van and leans against the hood. She starts mumbling to my van and occasionally cussing at it. Except for the curse words I couldn't tell what she was saying.

As she threw her head back to drain the beer can she fell over flat on her back in front of my van. I waited a few minutes to see if she was going to get back up, but there was no sign of her. I finally, quietly got out of the van to see what she was doing. She was flat on her back snoring out cold. I video taped her snoozing and packed it up for the day. I backed out of my parking space and left her there.

Hunting for the hunter's

In 1990 we did a lot of work for an insurance company that was based here in Atlanta. We got a call from one of our regulars regarding a large fraud investigation in Dalton, Georgia. The city is nestled in the foot hills of the north Georgia mountains in the northwest corner of the state. I had hoped the target lived in town, but as luck would have it she resided off a private road on a mountain top and she was surrounded by family.

This particular target was a middle aged woman who had a quite jaded past. She had been the subject of several fraud investigations ranging from workers comp claims all the way to the arson of her daughter in law's house. She had two ongoing insurance claims when I got involved. Previous attempts to surveil her by other investigator's resulted in them getting burned. I knew it would be a very tough case coming in to it.

I decided to do what I call "slow walking" the case. I carefully researched the target's property and that of her families including satellite photo's of the entire area. I needed to know all routes in and off the mountain top where they resided. Fortunately there was only one way off the mountain top and it came out on a state highway in a wide open valley. I found that I could set up approximately a mile from the road and have a clear view of it. With my most powerful lense on my camera I could easily ID any one coming out, without being seen.

After a couple of weeks I was able to ID most of her family members and their vehicles, but no sign of her and it was getting frustrating. One day while sitting on surveillance there, I reviewed the file on the case for the tenth time. I started thinking that if my target was the primary suspect of the arson at her daughter in law's house, they probably didn't get along very well.

I did a little research and a got her phone number. I crossed my fingers and dialed the number. She answered the phone and I introduced my self and then asked her opinion of my target. She really didn't like her very much and started providing me all types of information. She told me that my target was extremely cautious and on the rare occasion she leaves the mountain top she dresses as a man. She also told me she was an avid dear hunter and had an upcoming hunting trip planned. I decided it would be a great opportunity to hopefully catch her off guard.

I headed out to the hunting camp in the Cohutta wilderness area the same morning my target and her hunting party left out. It was a lot further drive for me so they should already be there setting up camp. After I got there I went to the ranger station and got a map of the hunting area which was quite expansive. I locked the hubs on my four wheel drive and started riding the mountainous fire roads searching for their camp. After about an hour and a half I located their camp. I pulled in to a nearby camping spot and started my "just another dear hunter act". My target was definitely out and about and having a good time. I was able to shoot a total of eight hours of video tape of my target doing all sorts of thing's she was not supposed to be able to do. This not only killed her false insurance claims, but also she was criminally prosecuted for insurance fraud.

Gee, no wonder he didn't go back to work

One of our regular insurance clients called a case in that involved a man that resided in Warner Robbins, Georgia. He was an employee at a large manufacturing company in town and alleged back injury. He just kept dragging the claim on even though no doctor could find anything wrong with him. They had tried to settle the claim for a reasonable amount, however his attorney wouldn't budge.

After my initial research on the guy I noted he had several previous arrests for possession of drugs and a DUI. It indicated to me he was a partier and that's good, because they're usually not real aware of what's going on around them.

I headed out to Warner Robbins early the next morning and got on location at sunrise. The neighborhood was in a bad area of town and there was a lot of graffiti on fences and buildings. I knew I was right in the middle of gang banger land so I would have to keep a very low profile, especially since I was the wrong color. My target's house was pretty run down looking, but he had several new high dollar cars parked in the driveway.

The morning wore on and all remained quiet. No movement or detectable activity was noted at my target's residence and little activity in general in the area. Finally, shortly after noon an unidentified female exited the residence and departed in one of the cars. She came back twenty minutes later with several McDonald's bags so I was fairly confident my target was in the house. I stayed on location until five p.m. without any further activity and called it a day. I checked into a hotel and went and had dinner. After dinner I decided to do a ride by of my targets residence and discovered one of the vehicles were gone. I made a pretext call to the residence and a female answered the phone and told me my target was not there. I made several other ride bys that night, but the vehicle never returned.

I started the next morning early as usual, but after few hours of inactivity I temporarily terminated the surveillance. I waited until four p.m. and picked it back up again and both vehicles were there. Shortly after six my target exits the house and departs in his car. I followed him around town for a little while and then he stopped at this grungy looking pool hall and shot house. There were quite a few unsavory characters hanging around outside and my target apparently knew them well. I parked where I had a good view of the front and side of the building where my target parked and began rolling video tape. It quickly became apparent that my target was a drug dealer. I videoed him blatantly conducting drug sales in plain view repeatedly throughout the evening.

The following day I contacted the Macon G.B.I. office and showed them the tape. They of course requested a copy of the tape and I made them one. Within a weeks time the G.B.I. put together and executed a sting operation and arrested my target and about two dozen others on various offenses.

The computer take down

I received a call from one of our corporate security clients regarding thefts from one of their distribution centers. In the last two weeks they had eight high dollar computers systems come up missing. They had reviewed the security camera tapes, but found nothing at all suspicious. It was as if the computers had disappeared into thin air.

I went to the facility to take a look around. It was actually several older buildings joined together and had numerous entrances and exits. The rear of the building was almost all a loading dock where tractor trailers backed in for loading and unloading. As I looked around I noticed several apparent blind spots where their security cameras didn't cover. One of the blind spots was at a locked exit door that was never used. This really stuck in my head.

Because of the layout of the area it would be necessary to set up covertly in the woods behind the facility where I had a clear view of the door in the blind spot. I could park my vehicle at an adjacent business and make the short hike thru the woods.

I set up before the employees showed up at work and got settled in. The employees parked outside of the fence surrounding the rear of the building and walked right past the blind spot to enter the building. The first day goes by and I did not observe any suspicious activity at all. I worried that when the computers were discovered missing our thieves may lay low for awhile.

The second and third day of surveillance went as the first. No suspicious activity at all. I started second guessing my theory on how the stuff was getting out and tried to think of something else I could do to get to the bottom of what was going on. But something kept telling me I was on the right track and that I just needed to be patient a little longer.

I set up the fourth morning as I usually did, settling in behind a camouflage net and getting my camera ready. About fifteen minutes before the lunch bell rang I saw the door in the blind spot open slightly. I immediately started rolling video tape and out pops this guy carrying a large box. He takes it to the rear of a mini van parked close by and puts it inside. Bingo, I got the son of a bitch. He apparently laid low for a while until things cooled off and was now back at it again. I contacted my client with my findings and they were ecstatic and asked me to take it a step further. They wanted me to bust him in the act.

I contacted a detective with the local law enforcement and told him what I had and wanted to do. He was more than eager to participate and we set up a sting hopefully the following day. I set up as usual and had the detective on speed dial on my cell phone. About the same time as before the door opens slightly and I call my detective buddy. As the guy comes out the door I start to move in. about the time I was walking up behind the guy my detective buddy comes flying in the parking area. We arrested the guy on the spot in front of all his co-workers making an example of him.

How to get a confession

I had a corporate security client that owned several different restaurant chains in the Atlanta area. We were in charge of responding to and investigating any theft or robbery that occurred at any of their restaurants. I would often get a call at night and have to drop everything and go to work.

I received a call from our client regarding a suspicious robbery at one of their locations earlier that day. Allegedly one of their locations had been robbed at the drive thru. I made my way to the restaurant and sat down with the manager before I started interviewing the staff that was present at the robbery. The guy that was allegedly robbed at the drive thru window seemed unusually nervous so I would just let him stew and would interview him last.

As I was going thru the interview process I discovered that there was no indication there was anything wrong until the drive thru guy turned around and calmly said he was just robbed. No one heard or saw anything until that time. Usually, a robber will yell and threaten to intimidate their victim; however this apparently did not happen. I interviewed a counter worker that was present at the time of the robbery. She made the statement that she thought it was a joke, because the robber looked like the guy working the drive thru windows friend. Another dining room worker stated he thought the car the robber was driving looked like the drive thru guy's roommate's car.

I finished my interview with all the employees except the drive thru guy and had a pretty good idea of what went down. Right as the lunch rush was slowing down drive thru guy had his buddy pull up to the drive thru window where he handed the cash off to him and claimed to have been robbed.

I finally sat down with drive thru guy and started the interview process. I always start with asking for a detailed description of exactly step by step what transpired. I will then ask for detail descriptions of the perpetrator and the vehicle. It became obvious that the guy was not telling me the truth because he couldn't keep his story straight. I kept pressing him on certain details and he got real nervous but maintained his story.

I took a break for a minute and walked into the rear of the restaurant. I found a nice private corner of the store room and went to get drive thru guy from the dining room. I walked up to him with a smile on my face and told him I wanted to show him something. I escorted him to the store room and faced him. I grabbed him by his shirt collar with both hands and slammed his ass against the wall. I looked him dead in the eyes and said "we can do this the easy way or the hard way and I don't give a shit which but you're going to tell me the truth now". He immediately confessed that he and his roommate set the whole thing up and I had him write a confession while I waited for the police to arrive. I then had drive thru guy call his roommate and tell him he needed him to pick him up. When he arrived I sent them to jail together.

Intercept in Tampa

I received a call from a very distraught lady whose eighteen year old daughter had been taken from the house while she was at work. Although the girl was eighteen she had a mental disability and functioned on the level of a fourteen year old and the mother feared for her safety.

The girl spent a lot of time on the family computer surfing chat rooms and social networking sites and had met a guy that went by the name of Raven. They constantly e-mailed one another for some time. The mother started seeing a change in her daughter's behavior. She was becoming more withdrawn and secretive and started spending a lot of time in her room with the door locked. The mother started snooping around in her room and started finding satanic writings and poems that this Raven guy had sent her.

The mother confronted the girl and forbid her from communicating with Raven any more and this only made the daughter mad and even more distant. A week after that confrontation a cab pulled up in front of her house and the daughter, carrying a suit case, got in and it left. Raven was in the cab. Because of her age the cops wouldn't do anything. The mother would have to get a judge to declare the girl mentally incompetent before police could do anything. Once that was done they could put out an APB and start looking for her.

During the week or so it took to get the judges order and warrants issued the daughter called a couple of times to let her mother know she was O.K. I traced the numbers down to several pay phones in a particular area in downtown Tampa, Florida. I felt certain they were staying in the nearby area. I contacted a missing persons detective in Tampa and filled him in. I then had the local sheriff's office transmit the warrants to the detective in Tampa.

I quickly packed and got on the road to Tampa. I was well on my way when I got a frantic call from the mother. She said she had just got off the phone with the daughter and she told her that they were leaving Tampa early in the morning to go to some sort of "Love Fest" in Ocala. I drove all night in some of the worst storms I've ever been in. I wanted to stop but I knew I would miss them if I did. My guess was they were going by bus because the Greyhound was close to where they were staying in Tampa.

I arrived in Tampa early the next morning and located the Bus station. I entered the waiting area and looked around for them; however they were not there at that time. I took up a position where I could see the exit, entrance and waiting areas. Approximately an hour later the girl and Raven walked in with their luggage and approached the ticket counter. I called the Tampa P.D. detective and he was on his way, warrants in hand. I met him at the door and we closed in taking them both into custody without incident. The girl was now safe and I could get some sleep. Mission accomplished.

You're going to pay for that

Very early on in my career as a private investigator I was working for several P.I. firms part time. I would also pick up bail jumping work from several Bondsmen around the Atlanta area. It was fun work to do, but sometimes it was more trouble than it was worth. Everybody wants to do the high dollar jumpers because your fee for the job is based on a percentage of the bond amount usually ten percent. Unfortunately to get those cases you also have to take the smaller ones for the bond companies you work for.

It had been a slow week for P.I. work so I went to visit my bondsmen to drum up some work. I picked up two cases, one was a ten thousand dollar bond and the second was a twenty five hundred dollar bond. The big one was worth a thousand dollars to me and the second was worth two hundred fifty dollars minus expenses.

I took the files back to my office and began the reviewing process. After carefully reviewing each file I started my research on their family, friends and known associates. The first place you start looking for some one is the people and places that they are most familiar with. That is where they are most likely to seek refuge.

On the large file the bond jumper had family scattered thru four states and I knew he would most likely be the most difficult to find. You have to carefully judge how much time you put into a file and still make a profit. On the smaller bond I was able to determine that he and his family all lived in a fairly small area in Dekalb County. I felt pretty confident that I could run him down fairly quickly so I started on him first.

I mapped out all the known addresses and headed out to have a look around. I started with his parents place and worked my way down the list. According to my client the bond jumper was very close to his sister so I decided to hang out around her house and see if I could see anything helpful.

An hour and a half goes by and my target all of a sudden walked out of the privacy fence and started down the street. I immediately started my car and crept up behind him. I pulled up past him and jumped out and pushed him to the ground. He was cussing and trying to fight me, but I managed to get him cuffed. I loaded him in my car and used a length chain and a pad lock to secure his handcuffs to an eye bolt I had in the floor board. I then headed straight to the county jail.

The closer we got to the jail the more belligerent he became. I tried to get him to shut up, but he wasn't stopping. He laid down on the back seat and started kicking at the rear passenger window. The third time he kicked he busted the window out and I went ballistic. I brought the car to screeching halt and jumped out. I snatched his ass out of the back seat and marched him to the trunk. I popped open the trunk and chucked him in face first into it on top of a spare tire, some tools and a jack. I made sure I hit every bump and pot hole I could find the rest of the way to the jail. After getting the window fixed I made less that a hundred bucks.

Be careful when you bend over in Dalton

I received a call from one of my large insurance clients regarding a suspected fraudulent workers compensation claim. The case was located in Dalton, Georgia in the northwest region of the state. It's a pretty nice place nestled in the foot hills of the mountains and just off interstate 75.

I headed out very early on a Monday morning. The traffic was light as I made my way thru downtown Atlanta and up interstate 75 North. I arrived in Dalton before sun up and proceeded to locate my targets residence and find a place to set up. My target lived on an older established road that had been cut in half by a new by-pass road thru the area. His residence was the last on the left at the dead end on the east side. I made my way around to the dead end on the west side of the by-pass and found a perfect place to set up at. Both dead ends were on high ground and I had a perfect view of my subject's residence.

The morning went by slowly, no notable activity at all except the sound of traffic whizzing by below on the by-pass. No one had come out of the house all morning, however there were five cars parked in the driveway and yard. I thought to myself that they were either lazy people or they possibly worked late in the day or at night.

Finally around one in the afternoon out comes a young guy and he started working on a car parked in the yard. He was too young to be my target, but I hoped my guy would come out and help him so I just sat ready and watched.

The young guy who I believed to be my targets son worked under the hood of the vehicle quite some time. It looked as if he was doing a major tear down of the engine and was stacking up a pile of engine accessories and engine parts.

About three O'clock a dilapidated pick-up truck pulls up and a grizzly looking guy gets out and walks to the house. A few minutes later Mr. Grizzly comes out accompanied by my target. They both waddle out to the car the kid is working on with their beers cans in hand.

They stood around watching the young guy work as they drank beer and talked. I shot video tape of it all just in case he did something that would be of use to my client. After about thirty minutes they move closer to the open hood of the car and stand behind the young guy to watch him work.

My target then gets right up behind the young guy bent over working and starts to vigorously humping his own son. He did this five times and it was the grossest thing I have ever seen. Talk about backwoods, it reminded me of that old movie" Deliverance". You should have seen the look on everyone's face when I played the tape in court.

Take your gun when you go pee

I spent a great deal of time on a large multi-million dollar fraud case in Chilton County Alabama. Over a course of a year and a half I spent more time there working than I did at home and got to know the area well. Many of the locals actually thought I lived there and I had my own table at the local steak house restaurant.

The only way to surveil my targets residence was from a heavily wooded horse pasture across the state highway. I spent so much time there I actually started giving the trees names to pass the time. I had to do something to pass the boring hours while I waited and watched for something to happen. Before you could head into the woods you had to spray yourself down with military grade DEET to keep the fleas and ticks from eating you alive.

I could only see the front of the residence that sat up on a hill, the driveway and part of the side yard from my vantage point, but it was the only workable location. If it appeared that my target was leaving in a vehicle I would have to run about a quarter of a mile to where my vehicle was hidden and try to catch up with him. Most of the time I was able to catch up and observe what he was doing, but it wasn't easy. There were a few times he left out and disappeared on me, turning off the highway some time before getting to the nearby town.

I had done this twice already this particular day in 110 degree weather and I was sweating like a pig. I always took a camouflaged cooler into the woods with me so I could stay well hydrated in that heat and humidity of the summer.

After a few hours of inactivity I decided to get up and walk around a little bit to stretch my legs. I was well concealed in thick brush and could move about fairly freely without fear of being seen and still see what I needed to see.

I had walked up and over a little hill some twenty five yards from where I was set up and decided to take a pee. You never pee close to where you are actually set up at to prevent attracting all sorts of critters to it and having to smell it all the time.

As I start to relieve myself I notice my targets two very large dogs cross the highway and enter the woods where I was set up. I had never seen them do that before and was taken by surprise, especially since I had left my gun with all the rest of my stuff. I hurried up and finished my business and headed for my stuff.

They saw me when I was about half way back to my spot and they started barking and raising hell. I hauled ass back to my gear and grabbed the gun. They instinctively stopped about fifteen feet away from me and just stood there barking and growling. I shot two rounds into the brush around them and they turned tail and ran. Just goes to show you that you can never let your guard down.

I wouldn't have done that if I were you

I received a possible insurance fraud case from a regular insurance client in Dothan, Alabama. It was your typical low back injury claim by a guy who worked in a warehouse. He had been employed there for about six months and was kinda known as a slacker by his co-workers.

After my initial research and mapping out his residence I was ready to go. I decided to make the long drive to Dothan on the following Thursday afternoon so I would be bright eyed and bushy tailed the next morning for the surveillance. I arrived in Dothan and secured a hotel for the duration of my stay there. I went and had dinner and then made a ride by of my targets residence to see the layout of the area and identify any vehicles present at his house.

The next morning I set up a little before six O'clock and settled into my hiding spot for the day. Before too long out comes my guy and I initiate a mobile surveillance and fall in some distance behind him. It quickly dawned on me that my target had an apparent new career as a self employed handy man. His truck was loaded with tools and various building materials. I followed him all throughout the day as he went from job to job doing various repairs at homes around town.

He even made several trips to a local home improvement store and always loaded what he bought by himself. I was having a great day because he was giving me everything I needed to bust his butt. He was a really busy fellow and worked until seven that evening before finally calling it a day.

After making sure he was home for the day I headed back to my hotel for a shower and some air conditioning. I got cleaned up and headed down to the lobby to ask the desk clerk were the best place to eat was. The clerk suggested a bar and grill down the street that was very popular so I headed that way.

I was seated within a few minutes and ordered my dinner. I tell you that place had the absolute best steak quesadillas I have ever tasted. Everything was prepared from scratch and seasoned just right. After finishing my meal I decided to have a seat in the bar for a night cap or two to celebrate my victorious day. I took a seat at the bar and struck up a conversation with the bar tender.

I noticed a guy seated with a girl in a booth not to far from where I was seated and he was obviously wasted. He was slurring his speech and being a little loud but not that bad. About twenty minutes later he started yelling and cursing at the girl sitting with him. She told him where to go and got up to leave. He then grabbed her arm and slams her back in the booth. I jumped up and grabbed him by the hair and yanked him out of his seat. When he got up on his feet I punched him square in the mouth and sent two teeth flying out of his mouth. As he is bent over holding his bleeding mouth I grabbed him by the belt and threw him out the door. Nothing pisses me off worse than for a man to hit a woman.

Be prepared

A while back I received a call from the president of a large trucking company based in the Atlanta area. He had very serious concerns over the security of proprietary information. It seemed that some one was providing his competition with confidential information regarding their accounts and contacts.

He informed me that there were only five individuals that had access to that information and he and his wife were two of the five. The third person was his son in law and the other two were long time employees. There was no known dissention with either of them so he didn't know what to think.

After examining the facility and how they operate I headed back to the office to do some preliminary research on the two long time employees. I discovered one of them was having financial difficulties and was robbing Peter to pay Paul. That in itself could motivate him enough to try and earn some extra cash under the table. He was their marketing director and handled the information that was being leaked daily so he sure had easy access.

I contacted the company president and advised him of my findings. I also suggested that we put him under surveillance and see if he was meeting with some one after work. He would have to be communicating with some one on a regular basis, because the information was very time sensitive and changes almost daily. He agreed and we started surveillance the next day.

After a week and a half of surveillance on this guy we had nothing. He left work, went straight home and stayed there all night. I had a strong feeling he was our guy, but he hasn't done anything out of the ordinary.

I contacted my client and suggested we bug his office and see what is going on while he was at work and he liked the idea. We made plans to meet at the facility at midnight the following evening so I could plant the bug. I prepared my gear and realized that I would have a problem with a constant power source for the recording equipment. I had planned to place the listening device directly over his desk so we could monitor his every word, but there was no place to plug anything up. So I called one of my best friends who was an electrician by trade and he was good to go.

My buddy and I got to the facility dead on time and the client was waiting on us. He let us in and I took my buddy to the targets office and explained what I needed. Twenty minutes later my buddy had installed a receptacle inside the suspended ceiling. It took me about fifteen minutes to install the bugging equipment and we were out of there.

When I reviewed the tape from the second day it all became apparent. He was spending more time on the phone passing information to the competition than he did doing his job. This is a perfect example of how being prepared and thinking things out can make all the difference.

Hanging by a thread

Back in the early eighties I did work for an insurance company that that had a lot of claims in the state of Tennessee. That was very much O.K. with me because I loved Tennessee and the beautiful scenery. I have been a mountain climber since the mid seventies and would spend almost every weekend somewhere hanging off a rock face before my daughter was born. I would usually receive six or eight Tennessee cases at a time and I would go up and work them back to back and be gone three or four weeks at a time. I would scout out a good vertical rock face close by and go climbing in my off time.

I decided to start taking one of my guys on these trips to show them how you do it efficiently and successfully. I had a new guy that was working for me and I'll call him Mikey. Mikey was a great guy and we worked really well together. He was interested in everything I did so he jumped at the chance to go.

We headed out the following Sunday morning on our way to Memphis, Tennessee. I usually started my cases to the west and worked east across the state until all investigations were complete and then head south to go home.

We finished our two cases in Memphis with great success having popped both of them and headed for Nashville to work our next three cases. We arrived in Nashville and decided to stay on the south side of town in the Brentwood area. It was a very nice area with just about every amenity you could possible want. There was a man made lake named J Percy Priest Lake not far away. It had once been a rock quarry but had been turned into a great recreational area. There were several tall exposed rock faces visible from the marina area and I wanted to go play on them when I had time.

We worked our first case in the area on that Friday and Saturday and we decided to kick back a little and take Sunday off. I told Mikey what I had in mind for Sunday and he wanted to go. He had no climbing experience at all, but he wanted me to teach him.

Sunday after lunch we set out on foot around the cove and made our way to the top of the rock race. It was about sixty feet tall and dropped straight down into the water. I thought it was a great place to rappel down and go swimming. I rigged the rope and taught Mikey the basics of rappelling. I then belayed him with a second line and talked him down to the waters edge. I zipped down behind him and took off my gear and jumped in. we hung out there all afternoon swimming and relaxing. Getting close to dinner time we decided to pack it in and get out of there. I instructed Mikey on the use of prussic knots and etrieres to climb back up the rope. He started out O.K. at first, but after he got about half way up he was exhausted and scared. He didn't realize how hard it was to go back up. As I was trying to calm him down and get him moving he flips up side down. He had neglected to zip up his backpack and when he flipped he dumped all of his gear in the water below and it disappeared from sight. It took me an hour and a half to get him up that cliff and he was shaking like a leaf. Mikey said I cured him of any desire to ever do that again.

Nothing you can do but hide

A few years ago I was contacted by a very nice lady who was very upset. She believed that her husband of ten years was having an extramarital affair with some one. She had overheard a portion of a late night telephone conversation he was making on his cell phone and she knew something was going on.

I suggested that we put her husband under surveillance and see if we could catch him in the act. She provided us with a description and tag number for his vehicle and a recent photograph of him. He had a very arbitrary schedule because he was self employed and often worked at home. She was an administrative staff nurse at the local county hospital and had a set schedule so I decided we should surveil her husband while she was at work.

The first couple of days of surveillance were kinda boring; he only went out to go thru the drive thru for lunch and to the post office to check his mail. No one came to the residence and he didn't meet up with anyone while he was out.

On our third day of surveillance on him, he was visited by a blonde woman driving a brand new Yukon. She stayed at the residence for several hours and then left. I contacted my client with a verbal update and she was very distraught. She knew of no one that was supposed to come by the house that day and didn't recognize the description of the woman.

I suggested to her that we should install a hidden camera and recorder in the house so could see what was going on. She approved the plan and I started pre–assembling the equipment. She was to set something up and get him out of the house so the equipment could be installed. I met up with her and she gave me a key to the house and instructed me that they only lock the knob, but never the deadbolt.

She set up a lunch date for the following Thursday and provided me the details. The plan was that I would wait for her husband to leave the house and let myself in and install the equipment. I estimated that it would take me about thirty minutes to locate an appropriate place to hide the camera, test it and get out.

Thursday came and I was in position at the appointed time. The husband left right on time and I waited just a couple of minutes to make sure he was gone, before I moved in. I parked my vehicle at the curb between their house and the neighbor's house. I grabbed my brief case full of gear and headed to the door. I put the key in the lock and unlocked the door. The door did not open the dead bolt was also locked. I tried the key in the dead bolt and it did not work.

I returned to my van and retrieved my lock pick kit. It took me a couple of minutes to unlock the dead bolt and I let myself in so I tried to hustle up and get the equipment in place as fast as possible. I located a perfect spot to place the camera on top of a book case in the hall and went straight to work. I got it installed and tested and was gathering my stuff up when I hear a car pull up in the driveway. Oh shit it was the husband.

I grabbed my stuff and scrambled to find a place to hide. I went into the den area and saw a closet and headed for it. I crawled into the bottom of it under the cloths rack and squished myself back into the corner. I can hear the husband walking around the house, but I wasn't exactly sure of where he was at.

About thirty minutes later he comes into the den and starts rifling thru a desk and a filing cabinet not more than two feet from the closet door. The only thing I could do is to remain completely still and control my breathing and hope I didn't give myself away. After what seemed like forever he finally left the room and I could breathe easy.

A few minutes later he comes back into the room and opens the closet door and starts rummaging around in the top of the closet. I sat motionless and held my breathe. My heart was pounding in my chest so bad I was afraid he would hear it. He finally closed the door and left the room. Damn, that was too close for comfort.

A few minutes later I hear the door slam and his car start. I waited a few minutes and proceeded to get the hell out of there. I was never so glad to see my van and wasted no time getting out of the neighborhood.

Fortunately, all that stress paid off. We were able to document the husband and his little blonde friend indeed carrying on an affair right in their home. They sort of acted like teenagers doing the nasty in different places all around the house even on the kitchen table.

My client was able to prove her case beyond a shadow of a doubt in court and received a favorable divorce settlement. Although it didn't negate the pain of the break up it gave her closure to a very painful chapter of her life.

Open the window first

I was contacted by one of my law firm clients regarding a case that was coming up on their trial calendar fairly soon. It was a medical malpractice case where an individual alleged several problems post operatively and was now suing his surgeon. The case had sort of fell thru the cracks and had not been investigated. They asked me if we could get right on it and I said I would.

I started the surveillance the very next day bright and early in the morning. It was a good set up so I could sit all day and never be noticed and I had a perfect view of his residence and yard. If he came out of the house for any reason I would be able to see him clearly and document any activity.

After the first couple of days of surveillance I contacted my client and gave him a verbal on our progress on the case thus far. We had not even seen the guy come out of the house and I was afraid he was laying low before the trial. My client has getting increasingly worried because he really did not have anything to use to defend his client and asked me to stay on it in hopes he would show himself and give him something to work with.

A few more days pass and still no sign of my guy. We were creeping closer and closer to the trial date and we still had nothing. Again I contacted my client and advised him of the lack of activity and suggested to him that we may have waited too late on this one. He was getting desperate at this point and requested we watch the target's residence twenty four hours a day for the next three days. Although I really didn't believe it would do much good I hated to turn away the business so I reluctantly said yes.

The first day I rotated eight hour shifts with my number two guy so we would have our guy covered. On one of our off shifts we would crash and get some sleep. The second day we did the exact same thing and still no sign of our guy. We were sure he was home because his car was in the driveway and we had actually spoken to him on the phone under a pretext. Thru the entire time we surveilled him he had only two visitors and we never saw them bring anything in or out with them. I figured the guy was either really in bad shape or he was a hermit.

On the last day of the twenty four hour surveillance I had to pull the last three shifts myself because my number two guy had a prior commitment that he couldn't break. I settled in for what I just knew was going to be a long day.

After about seventeen hours of continuous surveillance I had already filled my pee jug up and was starting to feel the urge again. I looked around and found a drink cup and promptly filled it up. Seven hours later and it is time to leave. I was so tired all I wanted to do was go home and pass out. I carefully picked up the cup of pee and sat it on the console and got in the drivers seat. I started the van up and drove out of the area. I reached over and grabbed the pee cup and tossed it out the window. One problem though, I forgot to roll down the window. It splashed back and I was covered with pee.

The really helpful realtor

Not long ago I received a case from one of our large insurance clients on a guy that lived in North Atlanta who was alleging an on the job injury. He was complaining of back, knee and shoulder pain so intense he could no longer work and was suing his employer for permanent, total disability.

I did my usual pre-surveillance research confirming his identity and address. Nothing unusual was showing up on him either civilly or criminally. I mapped out his residence and neighborhood and was ready to do the surveillance.

I started the surveillance early the next morning. The neighborhood where he resided was an older upper middle class area with big yards and lots of tree lined curving streets. I was very happy that it was a good set up for doing surveillance. I picked a spot and settled in for the day and documented the vehicles present at his residence.

The first day of surveillance went very smoothly, but uneventful. A female and a child were seen coming and going from the residence several times throughout the day, but no sign of my target. On one of the female's trips out and about I made a pretext telephone to the residence and it confirmed my guy was at home. I kept hoping he would show himself, but it did not happen.

When I came in the second day I immediately noticed that there were magnetic signs on his SUV parked in the driveway. I zoomed in on the signs with my camera and noted that my target was advertising himself as a real estate agent. I documented the signs and the contact numbers and sat and waited on him. After about half the day with no activity I decided to terminate the surveillance for the day and head to the office.

When I got to the office I had my wife (who is also a P.I.) call his contact number and pose as a prospective buyer. The guy fell for in hook, line and sinker and was soon e-mailing her prospective properties.

I had her play it slow and easy so he wouldn't get suspicious that he was being set up. A couple of days later she contacted our target and set up an appointment to look at one of the properties he had found.

We headed out to meet him so he could show us the property at the scheduled time. When we got close to the meeting place I put on my wireless cell phone camera and we continued on. When we arrived our target was already there with a big smile on his face. He proceeded to walk us all thru the entire property starting with the yard and finally ending up on the pull down stairs in the attic. He was up and down stairs, picking things up and generally moving around with absolutely no problems what so ever. He kept going on and on about the property and we thought we would never get away from him. When we finally got away from him, we high fived each other and went to dinner.

That will make you keep your head down

I was again preparing to make another trip out to Chilton County, Alabama on the on going fraud investigation I had been working on. It was the Memorial Day weekend and I hoped my target would be out and about enjoying the weekend.

Over the months of surveillance on him I noticed a pattern of in and out traffic at his residence. It was sporadic early in the week and increased as the weekend approached. It was indicative of possible drug activity and the nearby fire station had noted a chemical odor periodically in the air that they believed was coming from his place.

I had performed numerous day time surveillances on the target with some results, but I really wanted to know what was going on up on that hill when a large number of people would show up there and hang out. I figured the Memorial Day weekend would be a prime time to conduct night surveillance up there.

I checked and packed my night vision gear and camera and got on the road. I checked into my usual hotel about five p.m. on that Friday and headed out to my favorite restaurant in town. After I finished dinner I headed back to the hotel to change clothes.

I arrived at the target area about six thirty and drove my 4x4 to its regular hiding spot. I loaded up my gear and headed out thru the woods as I tried to steer clear of those lovable but annoying horses. I was in my usual concealed surveillance spot fifteen minutes later and settled in to await the evening's festivities.

Shortly after sun set the vehicles started showing up and driving out of view up the targets driveway. I waited about an hour in my hide out to let the party get good and started before I donned my night vision goggles and started to make my way up.

At ten p.m. there was loud music and voices echoing down from the target's place and it was time to go. It was a pitch black night and without the proper gear it would have been impossible to get up on the hill safely. I carefully made my way up thru the thick underbrush being very careful about my noise disciple. I knew the people wouldn't hear me, but it was their damn dog's that concerned me. I had already had a couple of encounters with them before.

I had moved about eighty yards up the hill and was just at the crest of the hill where his trailers sat. He had two single wide trailers positioned one behind the other about thirty feet apart. I continued to slowly skirt around the area to find an optimal position to settle into. As the group of people just came into my view, a burst of automatic rifle fire erupted from the area. An AK-47 assault rifle has a very distinct sound, you can hear the "clack" of the bolt as it cycles and that is exactly what that was. I made myself into a pancake and laid motionless on the ground as I tried to determine what direction into the woods they were firing the weapon. I decided to say screw it and got the hell out of there as fast as I could.

His wife didn't have a clue

I got a call from a lady that had become suspicious of her husbands behavior. He had become distant and preoccupied over the last six months and that wasn't like him. He had previously been very caring and loving to her and then all of a sudden he just changed. She was afraid that he may be having an affair with his secretary at work.

She provided us with all the pertinent information and a photograph so we had everything we needed to start the case. We decided to start the surveillance at his office at lunch time and go from there. If he and the secretary went to lunch together we would be able to observe their behavior toward each other.

The first day he came out of his office building minutes after noon and headed to his car. Although he was alone, he may meet some one for lunch so we followed him out. He proceeded to a local eatery and had lunch alone. When he was finished he went straight back to the office. We took a break for a few hours and picked the surveillance up again when it was close to his quitting time.

The target left work right on time however went in the opposite direction of his home and headed south to an area known as Midtown Atlanta. There are numerous shops and restaurants mixed with commercial properties in the area. It is also known as a popular area for the gay and lesbian community. As we proceeded south on Peachtree street we got caught in traffic at a red light and lost visual contact with our targets car. We did a search of the area; however we could not locate him. We called off the surveillance for that day and would pick it up the following day.

The second day of surveillance started out the same as the first. He went to lunch by himself and returned to the office promptly there after. When quitting time came he again left the office promptly and traveled south towards Midtown Atlanta.

I fell in behind him in traffic and stayed fairly close to him. I didn't want to get stuck at a traffic light again in rush hour traffic because it was too easy to loose some one in those conditions.

My target turned down a side street and I continued past to avoid suspicion. I circled around the block and located his vehicle in a secured private parking area at a small building. The address was displayed on the building; however no business name was posted. I found a place to sit and wait on him to come out. An hour later he came out, got in his car and headed home.

The following day I did some research on the building/business my target had visited the night before. It turns out that the location was a gay bath house where gay men went to have anonymous sex with each other. I cringed at the thought of how dangerous that was, especially for my client. That was the hardest verbal report I have ever given.

Psycho lady

Some time ago I received a case on a questionable workers compensation claim in southwest Atlanta. The entire area was pretty much a bad place with drug dealers and prostitutes walking the streets. Most of the neighborhoods were thirty or forty years old and were falling into a general state of disrepair and a bad element had moved in.

I did my preliminary research and mapped out the area as I usually do and got my equipment ready for the surveillance. I figured I would get on location a little earlier than normal so I could find a place to set up before the locals got up and active.

I slipped into the neighborhood the following morning and found the best spot I could to surveil my targets residence. I locked the doors and crawled into the back of the van and stayed out of sight so no one would know anyone was in the vehicle.

As the morning went on the pedestrian traffic picked up in the area. After the go to work crowd dissipated the lower forms of life started to move about. By eleven O'clock in the morning I had two guys leaning against my van talking crap and smoking crack. Just another wonderful neighborhood I get to enjoy.

The thing that struck me was that even in this obviously crime ridden area I never saw the first police car patrol thru the area. You would think that they would ride thru at least once to check for bodies lying in the street. Half a block up the street from me was a guy lying in a trash pile and I couldn't tell if he was passed out or dead. I never saw the guy move.

Shortly after lunch time I heard two people in a heated argument, but I couldn't tell where the voices were coming from. The argument went on for some time and then quieted down.

Ten minutes later it started up again angrier than before. All of a sudden a man comes out of a house several doors up and starts up the street. A few seconds later out comes a woman with a butcher knife and she goes after the guy. The faster he goes the faster she walks cursing him the whole way.

I suddenly realized that they were headed for an elementary school up the street and I immediately called 911 and started following them. As the male ran onto school grounds I flew past the enraged woman and jumped out of my van and drew my weapon. I held her at gun point until an Atlanta Police unit arrived.

I was really terrified that she may encounter a child and in her toked up frame of mind and possibly hurt them. I just wasn't going to take that chance.

The aerial recon that almost ended badly

I received a call from one of my large insurance clients regarding a medical malpractice case in north Georgia. It involved an individual that had undergone brain surgery as a result of a head trauma he sustained in a motorcycle accident. The man was claiming that the neurosurgeon botched the surgery and as a result he was suffering various issues including stroke like symptoms and incontinence.

I carefully reviewed the file on the case and did my preliminary research. When I mapped the area I realized that this one may be very difficult. My target resided on a remote private mountain top that adjoined a National forest and this really concerned me. If I couldn't catch him coming off the mountain the only other possibly was if I could surveil him from the National Forest if I could get close enough.

I headed out early the first day of surveillance and arrived in the area at sunrise. When I pulled off the main highway I immediately came to a locked gate across the road that lead up the mountain. I knew from my research that several other family members also resided on the mountain and that meant I would have a tough time identifying my subject or his vehicle. I decided to sit down the highway a ways and monitor any in or out traffic and hope I got lucky.

After the first day of surveillance I had nothing. I contacted my client and suggested that we should conduct an aerial reconnaissance of his property so I could at least identify his vehicles and get a look around. My client agreed and I set the recon up for later in the week.

The day of the aerial recon I met a buddy of mine at the airport. I loaded my equipment in the plane and we did our pre-flight. We finished our pre-flight, contacted ground control and taxied to our runway. We received clearance from the tower and we were off.

The flight up didn't take very long and we were on location in about forty five minutes. I handed the controls over to my buddy and started snapping photographs of the area. We maintained an altitude of two thousand feet and circled twice so I could get a good look around and we were done. We climbed up to approximately eight thousand feet and headed home.

On the way back we flew over the golf course at Lake Lanier and the place was really beautiful so just for kicks we decided to circle back and take a closer look. We scrubbed off some altitude and decided to have a little fun and buzzed a few of the golfers. We then decided we better get going before some one got our tail number and reported us.

We climbed back up to our original altitude and headed home. A few minutes later I checked my gages and thought I was seeing things. The oil pressure gauge was on zero. We slowly climbed a little higher and radioed the Dekalb Peachtree tower and advised them of our emergency.

We continued on a direct course to the airport hoping it was just a gauge malfunction. As we neared the Atlanta area the engine started to vibrate slightly and we knew then we were in big trouble. Shortly after that we started smelling smoke and we were both about to shit in our pants.

As we passed over the General Motors plant in Doraville the engine started vibrating violently and we shut it down. That was the eeriest silence I have even heard. We had emergency clearance and glided in a straight approach to our runway.

As we glided in we were afraid we wouldn't clear the power lines, but luckily we barely made it and then glided over the airport fence. We touched down and rolled to a stop. We immediately jumped out of the aircraft, breathed some fresh air and kissed the ground.

There was a long black streak of oil down the belly of the plane and we later found out that the oil filters had clogged because of improper maintenance and the oil lines had ruptured. We lucked out that day.

7722

DAT

4		

7722

AUTHOR Flindt, H. Walter
TITLE Memoirs of a real life P.I.
DATE DUE | **BORROWER'S NAME**
4/10/10 | Judy Henden

DEMCO